FROM EL]
TO EINSTEIN...

Answers to Questions

Mike Reiners

Feb. 5, 2002

FROM ELEPHANTS TO EINSTEIN...

Answers to Questions

RUDOLF STEINER

*Ten discussions with workers at
the Goetheanum in Dornach between
7 January and 27 February 1924*

English by A.R. Meuss, FIL, MTA

RUDOLF STEINER PRESS
LONDON

Rudolf Steiner Press
51 Queen Caroline Street
London W6 9QL

First published by Rudolf Steiner Press 1998

Originally published in German under the title *Natur und Mensch in geisteswissenschaftlicher Betrachtung* (volume 352 in the *Rudolf Steiner Gesamtausgabe* or Collected Works) by Rudolf Steiner Verlag, Dornach. This authorized translation is based on the 3rd, revised German edition edited by Paul Gerhard Bellmann, and is published by kind permission of the Rudolf Steiner Nachlassverwaltung, Dornach. The line drawings by Leonore Uhlig are based on Rudolf Steiner's blackboard drawings

Translation © Rudolf Steiner Press 1998

A catalogue record for this book is available from the British Library

ISBN 1 85584 081 2

Cover by Andrew Morgan
Typeset by DP Photosetting, Aylesbury, Bucks.
Printed and bound in Great Britain by Cromwell Press Limited, Broughton Gifford, Wiltshire

Contents

Main Contents of the Discussions

earth. Halibut and plaice. Flowers as bearers of light and roots as bearers of salt. How the earth feeds itself and how human beings feed themselves.

how they thrive in water full of sun and warmth. Shirt is chest system, coat is head system. Tails and top hat were originally combined in a coat.

relative rest and relative motion. Einstein's view that one can only say that things are relatively at rest or in motion. Strange consequences of Einstein's theory. Spread of theory of relativity. Debate about it with university professors. Size of human being is not relative but determined by cosmic space as a whole. Debates on gravity in Rudolf Steiner's young days. Early and late Einstein. Plateau's experiment. Theory of relativity has logic but no feeling for reality.

Publisher's Foreword

The truly remarkable lectures—or, more accurately, question and answer sessions—contained in this book, form part of a series (published in eight volumes in the original German)* dating from August 1922 to September 1924. This series features talks given to men involved in various kinds of building work on Rudolf Steiner's architectural masterpieces, the first and second Goetheanums. (The destruction by fire of the first Goetheanum necessitated the building of a replacement.) A vivid description of the different types of workers present, as well as the context and atmosphere of these talks, is given by a witness in the Appendix to this volume.

The sessions arose out of explanatory tours of the Goetheanum which one of Steiner's pupils, Dr Roman Boos, had offered. When this came to an end, and the workers still wished to know more about the 'temple' they were involved with and the philosophy behind it, Dr Steiner agreed to take part in question and answer sessions himself. These took place during the working day, after the mid-morning break. Apart from the workmen, only a few other people were present: those working in the building office, and some of Steiner's closest co-workers. The subject-matter of the talks was chosen by the workers at the encouragement of Rudolf Steiner, who took their questions and usually gave immediate answers.

---

* 347–354 in the collected works of Rudolf Steiner in the original German, published by Rudolf Steiner Verlag, Dornach, Switzerland. For information on English translations, see the list at the end of this Foreword.

After Rudolf Steiner's death, some of the lectures — on the subject of bees — were published. However, as Marie Steiner writes in her original Preface to the German edition: 'Gradually more and more people felt a wish to study these lectures.' It was therefore decided to publish them in full. However, Marie Steiner's words about the nature of the lectures remain relevant to the present publication:

> They had, however, been intended for a particular group of people and Rudolf Steiner spoke off the cuff, in accord with the given situation and the mood of the workmen at the time. There was no intention to publish at the time. But the very way in which he spoke had a freshness and directness that one would not wish to destroy, taking away the special atmosphere that arose in the souls of those who asked the questions and him who gave the answers. It would be a pity to take away the special colour of it by pedantically rearranging the sentences. We are therefore taking the risk of leaving them as far as possible untouched. Perhaps it will not always be in the accustomed literary style, but on the other hand it has directness and vitality.

In this spirit, the translator has been asked also to preserve as much of the original style, or flavour, as possible. This might necessitate that readers study a passage again, trying to bring to mind the live situation in which the talks were given, before the whole can be fully appreciated.

The blackboards on which Rudolf Steiner made his drawings were covered with black paper which could then be taken down and preserved. The drawings for the talks in this volume have now been published as part of the Rudolf Steiner *Gesamtausgabe* (Collected Works in German) and may be found in vol. XXVII of *Wandtafelzeichmungen zum Vortragswerk*, Dornach: Rudolf Steiner Verlag 1995. While it may be helpful to have these reproductions of the original drawings, it is not essential, as the most important drawings, done by Leonore Uhlig, are given as Figs. 1–24 in the text.

S G, May 1998, London

Rudolf Steiner's lectures to workers at the Goetheanum:

GA (*Gesamtausgabe*) number

347 *The Human Being in Body, Soul and Spirit* (New York/ London: Anthroposophic Press/Rudolf Steiner Press 1989)

348 *Health and Illness*, Vol. 1 (New York: Anthroposophic Press 1981) and *Health and Illness*, Vol. 2 (New York: Anthroposophic Press 1983)

349 Publication of English translation planned for 1999, Rudolf Steiner Press

350 Four of the sixteen lectures in the German edition are published in *Learning to See Into the Spiritual World* (New York: Anthroposophic Press 1990)

351 Nine of the fifteen lectures in the German edition are published in *Bees, Nine lectures on the Nature of Bees* (New York: Anthroposophic Press 1998)

352 *From Elephants to Einstein, Answers to Questions* (London: Rudolf Steiner Press 1998)

353 Publication of English translation planned for 1999, Rudolf Steiner Press

354 *The Evolution of the Earth and Man and the Influence of the Stars* (New York/London: Anthroposophic Press/ Rudolf Steiner Press 1987)

Translator's note

I have added a list of German names and terms that appear in the text, with indications as to how they may be pronounced. Reading the lectures aloud, in a group, for instance, people often feel they would like to pronounce the words properly, and I hope this may be a help.

Pronunciation of German names and terms

im Breisgau	im brice-gow (as in gown)
Burle	boorle
Dollinger	doll in ga (hard g)
Erbsmehl	erps male
Freiburg	fry bork
Gruenberg, Gruenberger	green berk, green berga (hard g)
Kaffeehaus	caffay house
Lehfeld	lay felt
Marienbad	ma ri en but
Marienquelle	ma ri en kvelle
Müller	miller
Offenburg	offen-bork

Anna R. Meuss, October 1997

1. Discussion of 7 January 1924

Pachyderms. Nature of shell/carapace and skeletal development

Good morning, gentlemen. We have not been meeting for some time. Maybe one of you has thought of something in particular that we may discuss today?

Questioner: The large ants to be found around our woodlands have a kind of honey or resin at the bottom of their ant heap. This is used for ritual purposes; Roman Catholic priests like to use it for incense. I would like to ask where this comes from and what it is made of.

Rudolf Steiner: Those resins contain the same material as is found in incense, and really have no other value but it is a way of getting one's incense cheaply. Ant heaps develop because with their formic acid ants also secrete all kinds of things they bring with them from the resinous parts of the trees where they gather sap. It is not a kind of honey, therefore, but a resin that has formic acid mixed in with it.

Mr Müller: I would like to go back to the bees, the carpenter bees that infest trees. In my young days I knew a case where all the wood in a forestry area rotted away and was not used. A master carpenter came and bought enormous quantities of this wood, which in the old days was always only used to make boxes. He used the wood for carpentry in new houses. A year later, people kept finding bees everywhere in those houses. These bees were such a danger to the structure that the master carpenter had to take the houses back after two years. All the timber work, including the rafters, had to be taken down. He had to take the houses back completely, buy them back.

Rudolf Steiner: That can happen, of course. Did the bees get into the wood in the timber yard or when it was still in the woods?

Mr Müller: It was sold by auction in the autumn, then used in the spring, and the bees came out in the summer.

Rudolf Steiner: Anything that may be extremely useful in one respect can also be terribly harmful in another. This does not go against what I said before, which is that these bees in the wood are something that is really needed. As I said, something that may be extraordinarily useful in one situation can on the other hand be extraordinarily harmful. Let me give you an example. Imagine a little boy who is short-sighted. If he is given glasses, that is necessary and can indeed be very useful. But if the other boys were to see this as something rather distinguished and decided to put on glasses as well, this would not be useful but harmful. And that is how it is. Something that is extraordinarily useful in one situation may prove extraordinarily harmful in another. That is the way it is.

Mr Müller: I'd like to go back to the bees again and things connected with our life and activities as beekeepers. My colleagues have complained several times that it would have been better if I did not read out what I want to say but speak freely. I have to say to them, however, that I have only been to primary school and have no special gift as a speaker. I am therefore not in a position to speak freely. So I am going to read out again today what I have written and not speak freely. About the bees, the queen bee. (Spoke about beehives and then referred to problems between workers and employers; going back to 1914, he expressed some dissatisfaction. Made a comparison: we, too, are a beehive in that situation, and so on.)

Rudolf Steiner: Well, gentlemen, it is difficult to speak immediately off the cuff about such matters. I expect we all know from experience that when such things are brought up and one discusses them on the spot the discussion has a different tone than when the matter has been fully considered. Let us therefore consider the matter carefully, that is, if we are to talk about it at all. We have time available again on Wednesday and I'll then ask the gentlemen who have something to say on the matter that we use the time on Wednesday for this. People have, quite rightly, spoken of the temperaments. The temperaments work in a different way if one has had a sleep in between. I do not mean that I want to remove the subject from the agenda, for this is not to say that I won't say something on the subject myself on Wednesday. But I think the way to do it is not to discuss the matter right away, when some people may get rather hot around the collar, but give it time, until Wednesday. I'll therefore ask you, gentlemen, to speak on Wednesday, if you wish.

For today let us continue with matters of science. And as I said, Mr Müller's suggestion will certainly be considered, and we'll say what we have to say about it on Wednesday. And I myself will then also say what I have to say.

You see, with scientific subjects it is relatively, pretty well possible for someone who knows the subject to say quite a few things even if unprepared. But the whole issue that has been presented here is something I would like to think through first. Is this all right with you? (Agreement.) Does anyone else have a question?

Mr Dollinger: A question that has often come up recently – it has been in all the papers – is that one never knows where dead elephants have got to, for their remains are never found. I would like to ask Dr Steiner if it might not be interesting to talk about this.

Rudolf Steiner: That is an interesting thing with those elephants. The fact is that remains of elephants from prehistoric times are sometimes found in extremely good condition. And the way those elephants from prehistoric times are found shows that these particular animals, called pachyderms in natural history, must always have died in the places where such prehistoric animals are found in a way—that is, they must have been preserved in such a way—that they were enveloped all at once in the soil that surrounds them. What I mean is that these thick-skinned pachyderms could only have been so well preserved because it did not happen that water, let us say, soil and mud seeped in gradually. It must have happened that they were lying in a cave and a landslide caused them to be enveloped in soil quite suddenly. The result has been that when that foreign soil had dissolved the flesh surrounding the bones, the enveloping form, which was firm in itself, preserved the skeletal structures extremely well. You find most beautifully preserved examples especially of these huge animals in museums everywhere.

This proves that these animals have the peculiar habit of withdrawing into caves when the time comes to die. Of course, the matter cannot be taken quite as strictly as you have put it, for all we can say is that very often—one does of course also find dead elephants—no trace can be found of an elephant that before had certainly been seen around. These animals have the peculiar habit of withdrawing into caves when they see death approaching, and to die in caves. You see, gentlemen, this has to do with the fact that these animals—and what you have said refers essentially only to pachyderms—have such an extraordinarily thick skin. And what does such a thick skin signify? You see, the hard parts of an animal are the parts most related to the soil. Your own nails are also most closely related to the earth. And an elephant's skin is such by nature that it is indeed related to the earth to an extraordinary degree. Because of this an elephant really feels himself surrounded by the earth all his life, meaning the earth in his skin, and only feels well surrounded by his skin. Now, within his skin the elephant is really continually dying. When death approaches—this is the peculiar thing with pachyderms—these animals feel this particularly strongly, exactly because they have such a thick skin. They then want to have more of the earth in their skin. Their instinct then makes them go into caves. People tend not to look for them in those earth caves. If they were to look for them there they would find more dead elephants in the regions where elephants are. They are not to be found in the open. What this fact proves is that animals have much more of an idea of approaching death than humans do, especially animals with a thick skin all around them, but also lower animals, small ones such as insects, for example, with their horny outer covers. And you see, when it comes to these small animals we have to say: It is not only that they feel death approaching, but also that they make all kinds of arrangements when they come to die, so that death shall happen in a place that is the best place for it. Some insects withdraw into the soil to experience death there.

You see, with human beings the situation is that they pay for their freedom by having really very little intuition. Animals do not have freedom, everything about them is unfree. But they have great intuitive powers. As you know, when danger threatens, an earthquake, for instance, animals move away, while human beings are caught completely unprepared by such events.

We may say that it is extraordinarily difficult for humans to enter into the inner life of animals. But anyone able to observe animals properly, anyone with the gift for observing animals, will always find that animals act in an extraordinarily prophetic way in anything that concerns their lives. And the peculiar habit we have spoken of is indeed connected with the prophetic life of these animals. But again we should not compare animals directly with humans when they do such things.

Here we may speak of something else connected with elephants. It will make the subject of your question even more understandable. You see, it has repeatedly been observed that a small elephant herd, let us say, was taken to water. Now it might be that a young rascal was standing by the roadside as the elephants passed and threw something at an elephant. For the time being the elephant would seem to be a patient creature who did nothing of the kind, and his reaction would seem fairly indifferent. But lo and behold, when the elephant came back, he had kept a hefty charge of water in his trunk. And as he walked back and saw the boy again, he sprayed the boy from top to toe with the water, before the boy could throw something again. This has been observed on several occasions. Now we might say: My word! The elephant is a lot cleverer than a person, for the elephant must have enormous wisdom to remember the insult the boy inflicted on him, keep the water in his trunk and then take his revenge.

Well, gentlemen, such an idea of the elephant is not quite correct. You should not compare this with human cleverness but with another human faculty. If a fly settles on your eye, here, you do this: you brush it off without giving the matter much thought. Scientists, who have all kinds of terms for things, terms that are not always easily understood, call this a reflex movement. You simply use a kind of instinct, a defensive movement, to brush off something that might be harmful to you. Humans do such things all the time. The brain is not at all involved in such actions, where someone merely brushes off a fly. Only the nerves that go to the spinal cord are involved. I think you know that when a person thinks about something it is like this: up here is the brain, and when he has seen something, for instance, the optic nerve goes to the brain, and from the brain the will impulse to do something goes through the rest of the organism. But when someone simply brushes away a fly which has settled on him, the nerve does not go to the brain at all—even if it was on the head—but goes directly to the spine, and the fly is brushed off without any thought given to it in the brain. It thus is the spinal marrow which brings it about that we defend ourselves instinctively when something of this kind touches us.

We human beings do not have a thick skin, at least physically speaking; we have a very thin skin. Our skin is so thin that it is actually transparent, for it consists of three layers: the inner one is called the dermis or corium; then comes a layer known as the basal or Malpighian layer, followed by the outer skin, which is quite transparent. We do have a skin, like the elephant, but it is extremely thin. The outer skin is completely transparent. Because we have a transparent skin we are also in contact with the environment with our feeling senses, and because we are in contact with the environment we human beings think inwardly and consider things. The elephant is also physically thick skinned, humans often are so morally. What does this lead to? You can easily imagine after what I have told you that an elephant is extraordinarily insensitive to his environment. Such an elephant really feels nothing at all, and everything he perceives of the environment is by sight. It is like a world closed off in itself. To enter into the heart and mind of an elephant is extraordinarily interesting for some people. Sometimes a person should actually desire more than anything to be an elephant, so that he may gain in insight. For you see, if a human being had the human way of thinking as well as an elephant mind he would be so clever that one could not even find the words to say how clever! But the elephant does not have the brain to be that clever. Because he is completely closed off in himself, his reflex movements, defensive movements, slow down. It takes a long time. If a fly had settled on you and you did not have the quick instinct to brush it away, the fly would fly away of its own accord before you got round to it. With the elephant, it is like this: he would leave a fly be, for the business of brushing it off would probably only come an hour later, that is how slow the reflex or defensive movement is. And what the elephant does with his trunk is nothing but such a reflex movement, only that it takes longer. And we cannot say that he thinks: That boy has insulted me, I must pour a load of water over his head. An elephant does not think like that. If a boy throws mud at you, you give him a clout on the ear without giving it much thought. But an elephant is a slow creature, exactly because he is a pachyderm, and it therefore takes a long time until he goes there and then comes here and puts out his trunk to give the boy a clout on the ear. But as he takes in water during the interval he realizes that his trunk is stronger when there is water in it. He wants to make his trunk stronger by keeping water in it. And he feels his trunk getting longer. He simply wants to use the extended trunk to strike the boy when he sprays him with a load of water. So this is what we have to consider. We should not simply ascribe human wisdom to them but need to enter into their inner heart and mind. Then we discover such things. And the situation with an elephant is that it is a creature closed up within itself and notes everything, noting above all everything that goes on inside it. Because of this the elephant also becomes aware of approaching death and is able to withdraw.

The situation is that there is really only very little animal psychology today. You know, people observe animals and discover all kinds of interesting things, as I have told you. But really looking into the animal's soul—that is something extremely rare today. But one needs to strengthen one's senses if one wants to get at such things, to observe life altogether.

Take very small animals of the kind one may find. Some very small animals consist altogether only of a soft, slimy mass (Fig. 1). This soft, slimy mass can extend something like a threadlike feeler from its mass if there is a little grain somewhere near. An arm is produced out of the mass. It can be taken back again. But, you see, such creatures secrete

Fig. 1

shells of lime or silica, so that they are surrounded by shells of lime or silica. Well, you cannot see very much when you observe such small animals. But there are creatures that are more developed, and with them you can observe more. There are creatures that also consist of such a slimy mass, but inside is something that looks like small rays if you look a bit more closely; and they also have a shell around them, and the shell has spines (Fig. 2). Everything that later develops into coral looks like this.

Take such a creature, which has a shell with spines and inside in its soft mass such ray-like structures. What is it? If you really go into it, you find that those rays inside are not brought about by the earth but by the sphere around the earth, by the stars. This soft mass is brought about by something that comes from the heavens, and the hard mass,

Fig. 2

or the mass with spines, is brought about by something from the inner earth. How does such a thing come into existence? Well, gentlemen, if you want to know how it comes into existence, you must see it like this. Here is a little bit—I am drawing it much larger—of such a small slimy animal. Through an influence that comes from a faraway star, a little bit of such a ray develops inside. As it develops, the influence from the star is causing quite a bit of pressure on the rest of the mass here. This then pushes even more strongly against the wall here. A bulge forms on the inside of the shell there, because of the increased pressure, and a spine is created in the surrounding mass of lime or silica. So that the spine is brought about from outside, from the earth, the ray, however, from inside, but due to the influence of the star. Can you understand this?

The structure that develops here inside is the beginning of a nerve mass; the structure that develops out there is the beginning of a bone mass. We thus see, looking at these lower animals, that nerves develop under the influence of the outer world circumference, which is beyond the earth. Everything that is bony or shell-like by nature—the lower animals only have bone on the outside—develops under the influence of the earth.

As we go on to consider more highly developed animals, we see shell development come to an end and skeletal development evolving, reaching its most perfect form in man. But take a look at the human skeleton. Looking at it you realize that the head can be compared to a lower animal, for it has a kind of shell. It is soft inside. That is a big difference from the rest of the human skeleton. Your leg and thigh bones are inside, and the flesh covers them. There the human being has taken the bony skeleton inside. In the rest of the human being the external skeleton is not as it is around the head but is taken inside. This is connected with the fact that the blood develops in a particular way in these higher animals and also in human beings. When you look at those lower animals, everything is a white mass. Even the substance that flows in them as blood is white. These lower animals thus really have white blood that is not at all warm. The higher the animals, and the closer we come to the human being, moving up the scale of animal organization, the more the human being, who remains light-coloured, has blood mass present in him. And the more the nerve is penetrated by blood mass, the more does the skeleton, initially an outer shell, withdraw into the inner organism.

We are thus able to put it like this. Why does the human being have bones developed as internal structures, the way they are in his arms and legs? Because he has blood mass entering into his nerve mass. We are therefore able to say that higher animals and man inwardly need the blood inside them and therefore outwardly take the shell inside. Is this clear to you?

We are then also able to say: such a lower animal knows nothing of itself; human beings, however, and the higher animals, know of themselves. How does one know of oneself? Because one has the skeleton inside oneself. It is because of this that one knows of oneself. So if we ask: 'Why does man have self-awareness, what makes him know of himself?' We should not point to the muscles, nor to the soft parts, but we must point exactly to the solid skeletal support. Man knows of himself because he has a solid skeletal support. And it is extraordinarily interesting to study the human skeleton.

Let us assume this is the human being, and I roughly put in the skeletal system (Fig. 3). Now this is extraordinarily interesting. Looking at a skeleton you have to realize it has been inside a human being. But this human skeleton is completely enclosed in a membrane. If I wanted to draw this membrane I'd have to draw it like this. When the human being is alive, the whole of his skeletal system is as

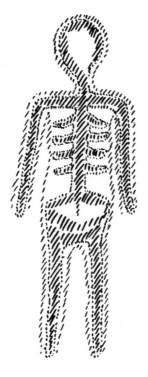

Fig. 3

though in a sack, inside a membrane called the periosteum, which fits it very closely. Imagine a joint (Fig. 4). Here one bone has a head and that fits into a cup, as it were. With the periosteum it is like this. There you have the membrane, with the whole bone enclosed in it, and the membrane continues like this, arriving there and covering the skeleton. So if you just think of the skeleton inside the human being, it is entirely separate in the human being. Between all other parts of the human being and the skeleton lies a sacklike skin. It is really as if you were to take the skeleton of a living human being and imagine you spread a sack over the whole skeleton, covering it closely everywhere, so that the sack

Fig. 4

would cover the outside of the whole skeleton. But you
don't need to do this, for nature has already done it. The
whole is in a sack, the periosteum. And the interesting thing
is that the blood vessels only go as far as the periosteum —
they are present in the whole of this membrane. This blood
nourishes the bone in so far as nourishment is intended, but
inside the sack the bone is all earth: calcium carbonate,
calcium phosphate, ash, salts, and so on. So you have the
strange situation that you are muscle, liver, and so on, and
have your blood vessels inside you, and the blood initially
creates a sack. This sack closes you off from the inside.
Inside the sack is a hollow space, and the bony skeleton is
inside this hollow space. So it really is as if your bones were
inside you, and you had separated them off, using a sack,
the periosteum. And those bones are entirely earthy, they
are earth inside you. You cannot feel them inside you as

something that is you. You are as little able to feel your bones, seeing what they are, to be part of you as you would feel a piece of chalk you pick up to be part of you. The chalk is outside yourself, and in the same way your bone is outside yourself, and you are separated from it by a sack. You all have something inside you, in your skeleton, that is not you. It is earth made in the shape of bones, calcium phosphate, calcium carbonate. You have this inside you, but it is enclosed in a sack, in the periosteum.

You see, gentlemen, that is not a place for something that is not of the spirit. For if you get some splinter of earth matter inside you, it must fester until it comes out. Your bone does not fester until it comes out. Why? Because there where you are dead inside yourself, where the bone appears dead inside its periosteum, spirit is present everywhere. You see, that was the wonderful instinct that made ordinary people, who often knew more than the academics, to see death as a skeleton. For they knew that the spirit was present in the skeleton. And if they thought of a spirit walking about, then it, too, had to be a skeleton. That was exactly the right image. For as long as a human being lives, he makes room in himself for the spirit through his bones.

This is something we'll discuss further in the very near future. But you also see from this that man does a great deal to bring the spirit into his bones. The elephant still leaves room for the spirit inside his thick skin. And because the elephant still leaves room for the spirit inside his thick skin, the spirit, which the elephant is then able to sense, is able to perceive when the outside world destroys it. Man does not know of his death because his skin is too thin. If he were thick-skinned also in physical terms, he, too, would withdraw into a cave and die in a cave. And then we would also say: 'Where do human beings get to? They go to heaven when they die!' Yes, gentlemen, the same thing which has

been said about animals has also been said about individuals who were greatly venerated by many people. Moses
is an example. It was said that his dead body was never
found. He vanished, and people thought this really happened in his case. He had grown as wise, people thought, as
I have been saying. If human beings were thick-skinned
physically and had their brains, they would be so clever
that words cannot tell how clever they would be. And
people knew of such things. You see, it is amazing what
people did know. They said of Moses that he was as clever
as he would have been if he had had a thick skin. And
because of this he withdrew, and his dead body was never
found. This is a very interesting connection. Don't you think
so? Ancient legends often have to do with a pure, most
beautiful animal veneration.

Well, we'll talk about this next time, if the discussion that
has been imposed on us today leaves time for it.

Until next Wednesday, then, gentlemen.[1]

2. *Discussion of 19 January 1924*

Poisons and their effect on humans

I'd like to add something to the lectures we've had so far, gentlemen. The next time I'll then ask you again to put a question or two on science.

I have told you that we must consider the human being to consist of a physical body, which we see before our eyes, and also of higher organizational aspects, which are invisible bodies. And I said that the first invisible body is the ether body. It is a subtle body that we cannot perceive with our ordinary senses but which is really the reason why a human being is alive, and essentially is also the reason why all plant and animal life exists. Another, yet higher body is the one we call the astral body. This astral body makes us able to have sensations and feelings. We have it in common with animals, for animals, too, have an astral body. But then, there is something in the human being which animals do not have, and that is self-awareness. For this we have an I. The human being thus consists of the physical body, which we see, and the three higher bodies: ether body, astral body and I.

The best way of seeing why people who have some degree of supersensible perception have good reason to say that man has these supersensible aspects—it can also be understood in other ways—but it is easy to see it if we consider the way poisons act on the human body.

When we spoke of the insects we saw that insect venoms can in a given situation have an extraordinarily helpful effect on humans. We saw that insect venom will get rid of certain diseases.[2] And this is also why medicines are mostly made of things that in ordinary life act as poisons. They merely have to be taken in suitable doses, that is, they have to be taken in such a way that they may act on the human organism in the right way. The action of poisons on the human body has its peculiarities. Just consider the following in this respect. You see, arsenic, which is sometimes also used as a rat poison, is a very strong poison. When a person takes arsenic, or if it is given to an animal, death follows immediately, or, if one manages to keep death away by giving the person suitable antidotes, driving the arsenic out again, as it were, a kind of slow arsenic disease may develop, and this arsenic disease then progresses slowly. Or it may also be that a person has an occupation involving something that must contain arsenic, and then arsenic poisoning with small amounts of arsenic may become an occupational disease. When it happens that a person does not take so much arsenic that he will be killed immediately, but takes a little arsenic, just enough to be harmful, he will grow pale, getting a kind of very chalky look; he'll grow thin and gradually die of emaciation. He loses his fresh colour and also all the fat that his body needs. The body gradually perishes, even if the arsenic action is a slow one.

But then there is something else. In Austria, for instance, arsenic is found in the rocks in some Alpine valleys. People start taking very small, tiny amounts of arsenic. They are able to tolerate this. They start with small amounts; then they go further and further, taking more and more, and in the end we have the strange situation that they are able to tolerate a terrible amount of arsenic.

Why do they do this? Well, gentlemen, most people do it from vanity. They get what they consider to be a beautiful skin colour and it makes them fill out more if they were skinny before. They take it from vanity, getting into the arsenic-eating habit from vanity, and this makes them look good.

So you get a strange contradiction. Such contradictions exist not only in human thinking—there everything usually contradicts everything else—but very much also in the natural world. There you get this contradiction: on one occasion arsenic makes a person grow thin and sallow, grey—not the hair goes grey but the skin. On one occasion the person fades away, the other time he takes arsenic to look good! There you have a complete contradiction.

What lies behind this? All you find in modern science about such a thing is that they will say: This cannot be explained; it simply is so. You cannot explain it unless you know about the supersensible bodies of man. You see, it is like this. Just as a human being always has to have formic acid in him, as I told you,[3] so he always has to have arsenic in him. He produces it himself. In many respects this may seem very strange, but you know, I have told you before,[4] when people say human beings can live without alcohol this is not true. A person can live without drinking alcohol, that is true. But he cannot live without alcohol. For if he does not drink alcohol, his own body will produce the necessary amounts of alcohol in him. All the substances that man needs are produced by himself. Anything taken in from outside is there merely to support, to stimulate. In reality man produces the substances he needs out of the universe. All substances exist in very finely divided form in the universe. Everything is there in the universe. There is iron in the universe, for example. Human beings not only inhale it, but also receive it into their bodies through their eyes and ears. And the iron people eat only serves to give support. It is largely eliminated again. If human beings did not have to live on earth from birth to death and therefore also do things on earth, they would not need to eat at all, for they could draw on the universe for everything. But when we work with our hands, or have to walk, we need the support gained from eating, for the body does not produce enough.

The human being is thus constantly producing arsenic; animals do it too, but plants do not. Why? Because plants have only an ether body. Arsenic is produced by the astral body, and therefore humans and animals produce arsenic. And what purpose does the arsenic serve? Well, you see, gentlemen, if human beings were not able to produce arsenic themselves they would not be able to sense things and respond to them inwardly. They would gradually come to have plant existence. They would begin first of all to dream and then to walk about like sleepyheads. Arsenic gives human beings the power to be awake and to respond inwardly to things. If I press down somewhere with my hand, it is not only that the skin is pushed in there at the front, but I have sensation. And this sensation arises because my astral body is all the time producing arsenic.

Someone who eats arsenic, takes arsenic, therefore strengthens the activity of his astral body. And what is the consequence? The consequence is that the astral body makes itself very much at home everywhere in the body. It gets too strong. It attacks all the organs and wears them down. And that is the consequence of rapid arsenic poisoning. If someone takes a lot of arsenic, quickly, his astral body begins to become terribly active, whirling, whirling, whirling and finally destroying the activity of the whole organization. It drives the life from the organs, for there has to be a constant battle between astral body and ether body in the human being. The ether body gives life, the astral body gives sentience. But there can be no sentience unless life is suppressed. To draw it in diagrammatic form, therefore, it is like this (Fig. 5). There you have the astral body, there the ether body. They are always fighting one another. If the ether body wins we get a bit sleepy; if the astral body wins we come wide awake. This alternates all the time in daytime life, but so briefly and quickly that we do not notice it and think we are always awake. In reality,

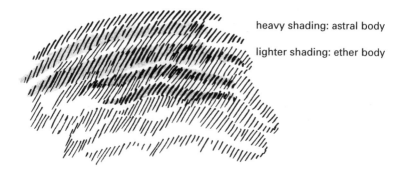

heavy shading: astral body

lighter shading: ether body

Fig. 5

however, being awake, asleep, being awake, asleep, and so on alternate all the time. And the astral body gets what it needs so that it may act down there in the right way from the amount of arsenic human beings produce themselves. If we give extra arsenic into the astral body, then in a trice the astral body gets too strong, much too strong, and kills all the life in the ether body. Now the human being can no longer live at all and he dies. But if I give someone so much arsenic that the astral body gets much too strong, the limbs, the internal organs, gradually lose substance and the person grows thin, begins to look grey, because the internal organs are not working properly. Yet if I start to give someone a little arsenic to begin with — one would not be giving it to him in that case, he would take it — the astral body begins to get a little bit lively, very little; it then actually stimulates the organs, and the effect is the opposite. If I give it too much from the beginning, it will kill the organs in a trice. If I give it just a little, it will stimulate the organs. It stimulates, just as when we use a spice. If one then goes up slowly, increasing the dose, the organs will tolerate this. The person begins to look better, fill out a little, because his astral body is more active than it was when he did not take arsenic.

But now imagine that someone who has been 'eating'

arsenic has to stop. Then his astral body will also stop being active, for it no longer has the arsenic whip behind it, and then the person will rapidly go into a decline. Someone who has started to eat arsenic and reached a certain dose is dependent on taking it all the time until he dies. And this is the problem. People cannot get out of the habit. The bad thing is that the person has to eat it all his life. Alternatively — but this is very difficult to do — one would have to reduce the dose slowly, giving less and less to eat. What usually happens in that case is like what happened to the farmer who wanted to get an ox out of the habit of eating with such a theory. He gave the ox less and less. The ox got very lean, but it still lived. Finally the farmer gave it just a single blade of grass, and the ox died. But the farmer said: Well, if it had given up eating that last blade of grass it would still be alive today. Yes, that's how it is with people who want to give up arsenic. They do not manage to leave off that last little bit; they perish before that.

You see, gentlemen, the human astral body needs arsenic, and it is strange to see the way scientists are groping in the dark today. They are really terribly in the dark! Today we keep hearing that a cure for syphilis has been found somewhere. A few days ago you could also read in the paper that a remedy for syphilis has been found in Paris. The fact is that no one knows what causes syphilis. It is due to the fact that the physical body becomes too active and the astral body is unable to intervene. But people do not know this, and they therefore keep trying one thing after another. And the funny thing is that all their remedies contain arsenic! You'll always find it, just take a look. But one can really only penetrate these things with the science of the spirit. All these things always contain some arsenic; but people do not know what it is about, they are completely in the dark. That is the peculiar nature of modern science. People will notice of course that something happens in a person when a preparation is used that contains arsenic. But they do not know that the astral body is getting more active, and that the physical body, having received such a principle of dissolution, will therefore dissolve. This is something a new medicine must bring about, that people gain proper insight into the human being again; only then can medicinal actions be brought in.

Now if we continue to consider poisons: some are mineral poisons. Arsenic is a mineral poison, for example, copper, lead, phosphorus, tartar emetic are mineral poisons; these are mineral poisons; one is dealing with stones, or with powders, powdered rock. So there are mineral poisons. Then there are plant poisons, for instance the poison that is in _Belladonna_, deadly nightshade, or the poison that is in henbane, _Hyoscyamus niger_, or in red foxglove, _Digitalis purpurea_. These are plant poisons. A third kind are animal venoms — we have discussed some aspects of these a short time ago,[5] so I only need to round out the subject today — insect venoms and snake venoms. And a particularly terrible, dreadful animal poison comes from rabid dogs.

We thus differentiate between mineral poisons, plant poisons and animal venoms. Each acts in a very different way on human beings. Let us take mineral poisons for example, lead, perhaps, or copper — all these things are toxic — or sulphuric acid, nitric acid, phosphorus and so on. Such poisons can really only be studied if they are not introduced into the human body in such amounts that they will immediately kill a person. For it is a strange thing. Taken in large amounts, the poison will kill a person, a mineral poison will kill. Taken in a weaker dose it will make him ill. The weaker actions are best for studying the effects of the poison. And if a suitable dose is given to a sick person, that person may get well.

Now it is like this with these poisons. When a person gets

arsenic, copper or lead into himself, the first signs are nausea, retching, then feeling sick in the stomach, in the intestines, pain in the gut, colic-like symptoms. This happens when a person takes mineral poisons. The body seeks to take in only what it is really able to digest. That is why retching develops as soon as mineral poisons have been taken. The person vomits. It is how the body seeks to help itself, but it is not enough as a rule. It will not be enough if there is a certain amount of poison and then one has to use antidotes. One must take care to get an antidote into the stomach and intestines so that the poison combines with it. The poison attacks the body when it gets into the stomach and intestines. But if I give an antidote, poison and antidote combine to form a compound. The poison no longer attacks the body, having entered into matrimony with the antidote, as it were. And after this I must give a powerful emetic or aperient so that it all comes out.

If you have weak poisoning—with more serious poisoning you have to get medical help—but what are the antidotes for weak poisoning? You see, a good antidote is this: quickly take lukewarm water and crack an egg into it, so that you have the liquid egg white and let this get into the stomach and intestines. The poison combines with the liquid egg white and can then be vomited up or be got rid off in diarrhoea; or, especially if the poisoning is weak, you can achieve this with lukewarm milk, also with all kinds of oils obtained from plants. These are antidotes to mineral poisons, except against phosphorus. If someone has phosphorus poisoning, one should not give vegetable oils, for they enhance the poisonous effect of the phosphorus. But all other mineral substances can be made to combine with oily substances and driven out. What happens when I have poison in my stomach? Well, the poison is there. Let us have the egg in lukewarm water I spoke of, and this will surround the poison in the stomach.

All these poisons I mentioned are also produced in the human organism. The human organism produces a small amount of lead, it produces a small amount of copper, it produces phosphorus. Man is the producer of all kinds of things. But these substances should only be produced in the quantities the body needs. If I introduce lead into the body, there is too much lead in it. So we now have to ask ourselves: what does lead do in the human being? Well, you see, gentlemen, if we were never to produce any lead in the body we would all walk around with rickets! Our limbs would go soft. And a child with rickets is indeed a child who does not produce enough lead. The human body must not have too much or too little lead. Generally the human being is able to produce the substances in adequate amounts. If he does not, he will indeed fall ill.

So if I now introduce lead into the human organism, what will happen? What happens with the lead which the human being is continually producing? Just think, you start to produce lead in your body when you are a child. But lead is not really ever found in the body in perceptible quantities, because we immediately sweat it out again. If it were not sweated out, then you would have had enough lead in you after a few years as a child that it could be detected. And now, as gentlemen of a venerable age, you would all go about with extremely hard rather than soft bones. You would only have to knock into something and the bone, being brittle, would immediately shatter.

So the lead a human being has in him, this small quantity, is always produced and sweated out again. If I ever introduce too much of it, it cannot be sweated out again immediately and destroys the human being. If I introduce egg white, which is protein, in water this will prevent the harmful effects of the lead. Why is that so? Well, gentlemen, the reason why I always sweat out my own lead is that I always also have protein in me. And when a baby drinks its mother's milk, one of the actions of that mother's milk is that by getting used to taking milk the baby also gets in the habit of sweating out lead all the time. I may also use lukewarm milk, therefore; it makes the lead find its way out of the body either by being vomited up or by being sweated out. The last remnants must always be sweated out.

So you see, we copy something which nature does all the time. The protein which is always present in the human being continually dissolves the lead. If I get too much lead into the stomach and then also put in protein in water, I am doing artificially what the body is always doing of its own accord. The situation is therefore that these mineral poisons and their actions have to be destroyed by bringing in something from the sphere of life. It must always be something from the sphere of life – the egg comes from a hen, and therefore life – or lukewarm milk, which comes from an animal, from life, or oils, which come from a plant, from life. I have to introduce something that comes from the sphere of life and still has something of the ether life. I thus cure the physical body through the ether body if there is mineral poisoning. The physical body is sending its substances too strongly into the ether body in cases of mineral poisoning. So that we are able to say: mineral poisons cause the physical body to penetrate into the ether body, entering into the ether body somewhere in the organs. So you see, if I have too much lead and it is not got rid of by an antidote in the stomach, if it enters into the body, then the physical body is immediately driven into the ether body everywhere in the human body. The physical body is dead, the ether body alive. But the ether body is killed by the physical body when this penetrates into it too strongly.

When I have copper poison and do not manage to render it harmless immediately in the stomach, using an antidote, it will enter into the body, and as a result the physical body will penetrate the ether body too strongly in the pelvic region. Again the body suffers damage. And so we may say that all mineral poisons cause the physical body to penetrate into the ether body. If I then give my antidote, something that comes from an ether body—egg white in water, lukewarm milk, and so on—the physical is driven out of the ether body again. You see, here we can see exactly what goes on in the human body.

How is it with plant poisons? If one has the poison from deadly nightshade, or from henbane, or from *Digitalis*, foxglove, or from *Datura stramonium*, thornapple, if one has some such plant poison, the following happens. In the case of mineral poisons one develops nausea, one's stomach begins to rumble, the intestines begin to rumble. But when one takes plant poisons—taken in large quantities, even alcohol acts as a plant poison, opium acts as a plant poison—it does not stop at nausea, retching, and so on, but the whole body is taken hold of. Hardly anything happens in the stomach with plant poisons to begin with. But further along in the intestines something happens, and diarrhoea develops. With mineral poisons, retching is more likely to develop, with plant poisons diarrhoea.

But it goes further. The body grows bloated, it turns bluish, and seizures develop. The black part of the eye, the pupil, opens out; it grows large, or it may grow small. So you see, such plant poisons intervene much more in the body. Mineral poisons only act on the human physical body. Plant poisons, coming from the etheric, from life, immediately influence the ether body. We may thus say that plant poisons cause the ether body to enter into the astral body. There the action on the body is a deeper one. While mineral poisons drive the physical body somewhere into the ether body, into life, plant poisons drive life into sentience, into the astral body. As a result the human being is narcotized, sensation disappears, and especially the eyes, being organs that convey more subtle sensation, are attacked, with the pupils enlarged or narrowed; the skin is attacked which we use for the sense of touch.

With plant poisons, therefore, the action goes more deeply into the body. And now one has to consider that just as the mineral poison was thrown out of the ether body with something coming from the sphere of life, the plant poison must be thrown out of the astral body. And here one has to look for plants that are more than ordinary plants, plants where the astral body has already intervened out of the cosmos.

You see, gentlemen, ordinary plants come up in the spring, they live through the summer and wither away in autumn. Those are the ordinary plants. But there are also trees. They do not wither away but persist for a long time. This is because the astral comes from the outside and intervenes. This is particularly so with particular trees. They do not become animals, plant nature has the upper hand, but the astral intervenes – above all in the bark. Trees characteristically surround themselves with bark, and the bark of oak trees and willows is most effective, because there the astral comes in most strongly. But all trees that contain tannic acid, as we call it, are trees where the astral has come in strongly. The result is that the liquid that can be obtained by pressing or boiling the bark of willows or oaks acts as an antidote, because with this one can throw out again from the astral body what has come into it through the plant poison. Coffee and tea also contain such an acid, in a sense, which throws the harmful influences out of the astral body. Strong coffee and good quality tea also have this effect against plant poisons. We can see now why it may not be such a bad thing to take black coffee with a meal on some occasions. When we take black coffee, the situation is – because plants always have a little bit of poison in them – that with the black coffee we throw out of the astral body something that consumes the body because the ether body has penetrated into the astral body. And drinking black coffee means that every time we put something into the body with a meal that makes it a little bit unhealthy, we remove anything that might be in the food and could penetrate too strongly into the astral body.

With tea one would have to be careful about drinking it with a meal, for it actually acts more powerfully and attacks the astral body. If tea is taken with a meal it mixes in with the digestion and encourages digestion, getting the astral body free again where it is involved in digestion. But if one takes tea after a meal, one gets directly to the astral body and makes it whirl around too much, be too active.

But you see, gentlemen, people have really had quite a good instinct. It is not for nothing that people have got in the habit of taking a bit a coffee, for that frees their astral body from something that is about to be harmful. The body always has a little bit of a tendency to develop poisons. Because of this the human being quite rightly needs these weak antidotes that are found in coffee.

You know that there are also people who want to encourage digestion not only with black coffee but by adding a small glass of cognac or brandy to their coffee. Well, brandy has something in it that itself acts a little like a plant poison, and this cuts off the astral body completely. The ether body gets particularly strong when people drink brandy. The ether body is particularly active when any spirits are taken. The person feels greatly at ease, for he has cut off conscious awareness and become all plant. He enters wholly into plant existence when he drinks spirits, and feels at ease, just as people normally feel at ease in their sleep. In sleep we do not, however, have awareness of that feeling of ease. When a person is able to feel at ease in sleep, this is because he is able to perceive the activity of the flesh. But normally people know nothing of being at ease when they are asleep. They do know about it, however, when they drink brandy. They are a little bit awake, but on the other hand their lower body is asleep, and with the lower body asleep while the head is awake they feel infinitely good. Drinking spirits therefore encourages animal and plantlike ease in people.

The third kind of poisons are animal venoms. There we have snake venom, for example, and the different insect venoms. Then there are poisons like the poison of rabies. These poisons act in the blood. It is easiest to see it in the case of snake venom. When a snake bites you, the venom enters the blood where it is tremendously harmful. But if you prepare a meal, draw venom from snakes and use it with pepper and salt, mixing it to make a meal—there is no point to this, for it does not taste good, but I mean if you did it for fun—your stomach would tolerate the snake venom with the greatest of ease. It is not at all poisonous in the stomach. Much the same holds true for other animal poisons, for instance insect venom. Only rabies poison gets into the saliva and from there into the blood, and therefore might also prove somewhat harmful if it got into one's stomach, though not as harmful as when one is bitten by a rabid dog. The rabies poison also gets into the blood from the saliva. But generally speaking we may say that animal poisons really only take effect in the blood and have no effect in the digestive tract.

You see, when the digestive process begins in a human being, the things he eats or drinks first of all reach the stomach. At that point they are still the way they were outside, physical objects, that is, still physical. If this is taken further in the case of plant poisons, which are not only physical but come from an ether body, it will go deeper. But all foods actually reach the blood. Snake venom can be properly digested; it does no harm when it reaches the blood via the digestion. Why? Well, when things are in the stomach, the physical body is still active. When they have moved along into the gut, and until they enter into the blood, the ether body is active, and in the transition into the blood the astral body. And in the blood the I is active. If you introduce snake venom into the blood, it causes the astral body to penetrate into the I. Mineral poisons make the physical body penetrate into the ether body. Plant poisons make the ether body penetrate into the astral body. Animal venoms make the astral body penetrate into the I. With animal venoms, therefore, there is nothing for it but to get it out of the blood again, for the I is the highest principle. There it is no longer possible to give something that will throw it out; one has to remove it directly. It means we can only get it out with something that is actually in the blood itself. If one has got the poison from a rabid dog in one's blood, or snake venom, one must take an animal and inoculate that animal with the particular poison. If the animal dies, well, then it has perished because of the poison. If it does not die, however, its blood is able to fight the poison. If one takes the fluid from such blood and inoculates the person suffering from rabies with it, he will have blood in him that can fight the poison, and in this way it may be possible to cure him. In this case, therefore, the poison can only be got rid of by its own antidote which is produced in the blood.

There is a great deal to be learned from animal venoms. For you see, gentlemen, human beings also produce these themselves all the time. Everything that exists is also produced by the human being himself. And it is because they produce such venoms that animals really have their powers; they would be stupid, dumb if they did not produce venoms. And man produces poisons very similar to animal venoms, doing so in organs that are more towards the head, but again does so only to a slight degree, so that his body is able to use them. If he produces them too strongly, he may actually have too much of those animal venoms in his own organism.

This is the case with diphtheria, for instance. Diphtheria develops because the individual produces animal venoms in himself. And diphtheria can be cured in a similar way, by inoculating an animal that can tolerate it with diphtheria, and then inoculating the human being with the animal's blood juice. He then gets something in his blood that fights the diphtheria poison.

You can see from this that there must be in nature not only things that are useful in a sense; things that are harmful clearly also have their function. Mineral poisons are the same, only more so, as something the ether body has to deal with in the human being. Plant poisons are the same as something the astral body has to deal with all the time in the human being. Animal venoms are the same as something the I has to deal with all the time. So we may say: some degree of poisoning is ever present in the waking human being — in the sleeping human being, too — but this poison also has its antidotes within it. And the situation truly is that we have to see clearly that poison and non-poison must be present in nature, so that the whole economy of nature can function properly.

And now you will also understand why I said formic acid has to be present. Formic acid evaporates continually from the ant heap, going out into the natural world at large. Because of this, formic acid is really always present everywhere. Human beings produce their own formic acid. But nature needs ants to produce formic acid that goes outside themselves. And if the formic acid were not produced, our earth could never be renewed in the universe but would die.

You see, when you have a human corpse, a poison called ptomaine develops in this human corpse, which is yet another poison. But human beings continually carry this corpse around with them. The poison is being produced all the time. If you have a living person, the physical body also produces ptomaine, but the etheric body, astral body and I are still present. They concern themselves with this poison all the time, consuming it, living on the fact that such poisons exist. If we were not poisonous as corpses, we would be unable to be human when alive. You can see from this that something must have gone away when a person dies. This is his supersensible aspect. And then, with the supersensible aspect gone away, the poison is no longer destroyed and remains in the human being. If people were able to think properly about the reason why ptomaine develops in the physical body, they would say: 'Yes, the physical body has been producing ptomaine all the time; there is no reason why it should not produce it, for as a physical body it is the same whether the person has died or lived. But the human being, the supersensible human being who needs ptomaine in order to live, has gone away; the ptomaine thus remains.' This shows, therefore, that the supersensible human being exists inside the physical human being. Modern scientists are unable to discover this, however, because people do not think in modern science.

So this is the general message, I would say, to be learned from the action of poisons. But at the same time you also see that if one wants to speak about the human being in medical terms, wanting to know of a medicine, one must be able to ask oneself: 'How does this medicine act?' There may be situations where one finds that the astral body is unable to work properly, is unable to gain mastery of the physical body and the ether body, and one has to give the person a little arsenic, for given to the astral body this will strengthen the astral body. And it is the same if one finds that the I is not working properly. One sees this when people develop gout or rheumatism, with the I getting too weak and unable to dissolve the foods. They then enter into the blood and become foreign bodies. If gout or rheumatism indicate that the bodies become foreign bodies, one has to strengthen the

I. This can be done with insect venom. If a bee stings a person, this happens naturally, and the person may be fortunate enough to be cured. Knowledge of medicines means: How does nature act on the I? How does nature act on the astral body? How does nature act on the ether body? We need to know supersensible nature if we want to have knowledge of medicines.

So you see, genuine knowledge is only gained in a particular field if we are able to consider the supersensible human being. All kinds of questions will no doubt come to your minds or may already have done so. We'll continue with that at nine o'clock next Wednesday.

1 *Mineral poisons make the physical body penetrate into the ether body.*

2 *Plant poisons make the ether body penetrate into the astral body.*

3 *Animal venoms make the astral body penetrate into the I.*

3. Discussion of 23 January 1924

Nutrition

I'd like to add something to what I said last Saturday. I can answer the two questions I have been given for today the next time. We have been speaking of poisons and their actions on human beings, and have learned from those poisons that for genuine knowledge we must rise to the supersensible aspect, to the spiritual aspects of the human being.

Today I'd like to complete the picture and add something to the discussion of elements that have such powerful poisonous effects. This concerns the work done by a more or less healthy body in nutrition. I have spoken on nutrition on a number of occasions,[6] but let us speak again of some aspects relating to nutrition, taking into account what was said the last time.

To feed himself, man mainly takes in three or four kinds of foods. The first is protein, which you can get to know most easily by looking at a hen's egg. Protein is produced in plants as well as in animal and human bodies. Both human and animal bodies need not only the powers they have in them to produce protein, for every living body actually produces protein; they also need the protein which a plant produces quite independently. And the human body also takes in animal protein. Some scientists have suffered severe embarrassment very recently concerning this very protein. Twenty years ago it was still taught everywhere that people had to consume at least 120 grams of protein a day to stay healthy. The whole of nutrition was therefore geared to it that dishes were recommended which people should eat in order to have the right amount of protein; 120 grams were thought to be necessary.

Today scientists have completely abandoned that idea. They know that people do not serve their health by eating so much protein but actually serve their ill-health, with the greater part of the protein going putrid in the human intestinal organism. Consuming 120 grams of protein a day, therefore, the human organism constantly has something like rotting eggs in its gut, that pollutes the intestinal contents most dreadfully, sweating out poisons which then enter into the organism, into the body. This not only produces something in the body that later on in life causes hardening of the arteries, as it is called — most of this comes from eating too much protein — but also making people highly susceptible to infection with all kinds of infectious diseases. People are less at risk of catching infectious diseases — they must, of course, have the necessary amount — the less excess protein they consume. Anyone taking at lot of protein will more easily catch infectious diseases — diphtheria, smallpox — than someone who does not take in so much protein.

It is strange indeed that scientists are now saying people do not need 120 grams of protein but only 20 to 50 grams. This, they say, is the amount people really need every day. So quickly have scientists changed their views in two decades. So you see how much store you may set by anything said to have been scientifically established. For if it should happen that you need to find out about the subject and you take a 20-year-old encyclopaedia, you will read in the relevant chapter that you should have 120 grams of protein. If you consulted a later edition you would read: 20 to 50 grams, and that it will make you ill to take more. So you see how it is, basically, with scientific truths. You are informed what you should consider to be true or false, depending on the edition of the encyclopaedia you consult.

All this shows that this simply is not the way to get a clear picture about things that involve the spiritual dimension.

And it gives us reason, if we really think about it, to enter into the spiritual aspects if we want to understand what happens when people consume protein. But this is the food that absolutely must still be processed in the intestines, in the lower body, and the lower body itself must have the power to digest this protein. You know that protein, especially fresh egg white, is semi-fluid. All protein is semi-fluid. Anything semi-fluid is accessible to the human ether body. The human ether body cannot do anything with solid matter, only with fluid matter. Human beings must therefore take all the food they consume in fluid form.

You will say that when people take salt, sugar, or the like, they are solid. Yes, but they are immediately dissolved. That is why we have saliva. The solid matter of which the actual physical body is made must never come into the human body from the outside world. From this you may learn: you have solid matter in you. You know that. Your bones are solid. But it is like this: the solid bones are created out of the fluid element in the human body; no solid from the outside world can ever enter into the human body. The human body must let all its solid parts arise out of the fluid sphere. You are thus able to say: we have solid matter in us and this is our physical body, but the physical body is wholly and entirely created out of the fluid sphere, and for the fluid sphere we have the ether body, a subtle body that cannot be seen but is present everywhere in the human being.

Protein must also be completely converted by the ether body, and this happens in the lower body. The higher aspects of the human being are also active there, as I have told you, but the protein must be processed in the ether body. The fluid sphere thus exists for the human ether body. And by merely knowing that protein has to be converted in the lower human body, you are able to realize that protein cannot have the hardest task in the human being, for it does not have to act up into the chest, it does not have to work up into the human head. You can see from this that protein cannot be a food of prime importance. We may say that people cannot possibly eat too little protein, for it is processed immediately in the lower body; it does not have to do much work. Protein is processed in the lower body. Even if people have a diet that is very low in protein, all the protein is processed immediately.

We can see, therefore, that human beings are perfectly able to manage with little protein. Scientists will now admit this, but years ago children in particular were fed excessive amounts of protein. And you know we see those children who in the 1870s and 1880s were given too much protein going about with hardening of the arteries, or they have already died of hardening of the arteries. The harmfulness of something does not show immediately, it only shows itself much later.

The second kind of foods are the fats. The fats we eat will of course also reach the lower body. But fats pass through the intestines and act most strongly on the middle human body, on the chest. For the middle body, the chest region, for proper nutrition of the heart, chest, and so on, it is therefore absolutely necessary to take in fatty substances.

We see from this that human beings above all need fatty substances in the chest region because that is the region where we breathe. What does this mean? It means that carbon, which we have in us, combines with oxygen. When carbon combines with oxygen we need to supply heat. What the fats do, when they themselves combine with oxygen, is to produce heat. Fats therefore contribute a great deal specifically to what is needed in the chest region.

Now we may say that proteins have a tendency to putrefy if they are not processed in the body, in the lower body. To have proteins in us that cannot be properly digested actu- ally means that we have something like rotten eggs in our gut. I think you know the stink of rotten eggs, gentlemen, and the situation is that when people take too much protein they sweat out this stink of rotten eggs into their internal organism. They fill themselves with this stink of rotten eggs. If you leave eggs for some time they become rotten eggs, and they stink like rotten eggs. And the part that has not been digested in the body will of course also produce a stink in the body; the other part, which is digested, will not produce a stink but enter cleanly into the body. And that is the work of the ether body. The ether body exists to overcome and remove the rotten stink that develops. The way it is in the human body is that the ether body fights and overcomes the rotting process. The rotting process is overcome by the ether body in the human being. When a human being no longer has an ether body after death, he begins to rot away. So there you have it right in front of your nose, we might say, that a human being does not rot away while he is alive; as soon as he no longer lives, he rots. Why is that so? Because the ether body has gone when a person is dead. The ether body is therefore the part of the human being that prevents rotting. We therefore have a continuous battle going on inside us against rotting away, and it is the ether body which fights that battle in us.

I think, gentlemen, you only need to think this through and you'll see very clearly, just from the evidence of your eyes, that there must be an ether body, that in fact there has to be an ether body everywhere. For proteins are produced everywhere on earth, and they rot. The earth would have to stink to high heaven if the ether did not keep driving this rotting principle away. Both inside and outside the human organism, the ether fights against proteins going rotten all the time. This is something we must certainly consider.

When we come to the fats, we have to say that fats do not rot but go rancid—you all know this, if you have ever left fats somewhere outside; even butter will go rancid. Fats thus have the property of going rancid. Now if you have left butter to stand, you will not be able to say if it is rancid or good fresh butter unless you have developed an eye for it. But when you taste it on your tongue you will know right away that it is rancid. This has something to do with awareness, therefore, with sensation. Rotting has to do with our sense of smell, with something you can smell outside. It is different, of course, if you have rotten eggs or the scent of roses, but in either case you smell it. Not so the going rancid. Going rancid is something where we only put a name to it because of something more inward, our sense of taste.

This immediately shows that it has a lot more to do with an inner response than in the case of eggs going rotten. The middle human body, the chest body, has to do with everything that is an inner response coming to awareness; and spiritually it is the astral body. As you know, in the chest we have something that functions on an airy principle. We breathe in air. We transform air. The air has its rightful place in the chest. In the remaining part of the human body gases and types of air should only be produced sparingly. If too much gas is produced in the gut, pathological flatulence develops, and that is not healthy. The middle human body exists for the generation of gases. And the higher supersensible spiritual aspect which intervenes here — it intervenes in things that are gaseous by nature — is the human astral body. This fights the going rancid of fats in itself. Just as the ether body combats the rotting of proteins, so does the astral body combat the going rancid of fats. People would continually have rancid eructations from their own fats, they would taste rancid to themselves inwardly, if their astral bodies did not constantly fight this process of going rancid. We thus have this astral body inside us to prevent fats going rancid.

You see, gentlemen, this is truly marvellous, for you can see from this that things go very differently in the ordinary physical world outside than they do inside us. Out there in the physical world fats inevitably go rancid. Human beings are blessed in that they do not go rancid, or only if they develop an internal disease. The matter is, therefore, that in health human beings have their astral body so that they cannot go rancid. They only go rancid if they eat too much fat, so that the astral body is unable to cope, or if something or other causes too much fat to be produced; cannibals know more about this than we do. Inwardly, however, human beings do perceive it if they go rancid. We may say that if someone grows very rancid, which means that his astral body is not sufficiently active, he continually has an unpleasant taste in his mouth. This unpleasant taste in turn affects the stomach. And in this roundabout way people get diseases of the stomach and intestines from the rancid fat in them.

If you notice that a person is inwardly going rancid, then arsenic is a good medicine for fats he has inside him which are not digested. Arsenic prevents one getting fat; it strengthens the astral body. The result is that a person is then able to combat the process of going rancid. These things are extraordinarily important. When a person shows himself to have an inner tendency of being unable to overcome his rotting protein with the help of the ether body, some copper compound or other usually proves highly effective as a medicine. Copper is thus effective when abdominal diseases, intestinal diseases are caused directly by protein. But when you find that something comes to awareness in the mouth, in the taste, it will not help to give copper; in that case it has to be arsenic, because you must first of all strengthen the astral body. It will not do to say simply that diseases of one kind or another are in a particular part of the human being. You have to know where they come from, if they come from rotting protein in the gut or fats that have gone rancid and affect the intestines and the stomach via the taste in one's mouth.

You see, therefore, gentlemen, that inside us we have the opposite of what these substances show themselves to be on the outside. We have an astral body that combats the going rancid of fats, while the ordinary physical and material world simply makes fats go rancid.

A third food people eat are the substances known as carbohydrates. Carbohydrates are found particularly in potatoes, for instance, in lentils and beans, and of course in all cereal grains. The carbohydrates are in there. Very many of them also contain actual sugar, which we always take as a food, or the sugar is directly produced from those carbohydrates because we transform the substances we take in when we eat potatoes, for instance. Potatoes contain much starch. This sticky starch is converted to dextrin inside us and then into sugar. If you eat potatoes you are therefore really taking sugar, for the potato starch paste is converted to sugar in the human body. As you know, grapes are particularly rich in sugar, hence also the alcohol. Everything alcohol is to man is, apart from being alcohol, really due to its sugar content, for sugar is produced particularly from alcohol in the human organism.

The first kind of food thus was protein, the second kind fats and the third starch, sugar. We have seen that protein is digested in certain quantities, without going putrid, by the ether body. Fats are digested, without going rancid, by the astral body. Now to starch and sugar. Looking at the ether body we have to say it is mainly active in the lower body. The astral body is mainly active in the chest region. Now we come to something else. You all know—I won't say from personal experience, but from seeing people who are not like you—the effects of alcohol, and you know that alcohol causes a peculiar condition in people, first of all drunkenness, but we'll leave that aside for the moment. But as you know, the next day — we have spoken of this before[7] — one has a thick head, a hangover, as it is called. What does such a heavy head or hangover signify?

Well, gentlemen, you can see even the term 'thick head' refers to the human head. And if you have heard people — different from yourselves, of course — talk about the bit of a hangover they had the day before, you will hear them complain above all of their skulls. The skull aches, and if it did not ache it felt as if it would drop off their shoulders, and so on. What is really going on?

The function of the head is to combat what starch and sugar want. What do starch and sugar want? You only have to consider wine. As you know, the wine, the grapes, are harvested when autumn comes. They are pressed and the matter then ferments. When fermentation is complete, people drink the wine. By becoming wine through fermentation, wine has overcome the fermentation. But if you put wine into your stomach, something develops from it that becomes part of the food again. The alcohol is literally converted back. Now starch and sugar are substances that want to ferment. Starch and sugar mainly want to ferment in the human organism. If you drink alcohol, the alcohol drives away the powers in the head that prevent the fermentation of sugar and starch in the human being. Let us take a good look at this. Let us say you had potatoes on 22 January, you had some beans and you drank alcohol with them. Right then. If you had not taken alcohol your head would have remained sober. Potatoes and beans contain starch and the sugar that comes from starch. The head would have the power to prevent fermentation of the starch and sugar in the proper way. If you bring in alcohol, the head loses the ability to prevent the fermentation of the starch and sugar you have in you from the potatoes, and then the potatoes and beans, and other things, too, cereal grains, for example, begin to ferment inside you.

Instead of being prevented, fermentation occurs in the person. It occurs because of the inability of the head that has developed because of the alcohol, so that the person comes to be full of fermentative powers. In central Germany, in Thuringia, people have a strange popular expression. When someone talks nonsense people in Thuringia say: 'He ferments.' It is not something people say in this area, but those who have been to Germany will no doubt have heard it in central Germany. And when someone is talking nonsense all the time, people in central Germany, in Thuringia, call him 'an old wretch in ferment'. The situation is that in central Germany, people connect fermentation with confusion in the head, with fooling around. That is an excellent popular instinct. They know that when someone talks a lot of nonsense he is in ferment in his head. And if someone has been drinking and got a thick head, he does not talk nonsense, for he tends to be quiet, but the nonsense is inside him, it rumbles in him. The process which develops to prevent the fermentation of starch and sugar is therefore the opposite of the tangible effect of alcohol. We may say, therefore, that there is something in the human head that continually works in the direction of preventing the fermentation of everything the person has in him by way of starch and sugar.

No one will deny that the I, the actual human I, has its main seat in the head, just as the ether body has its seat in the lower part and the astral body in the middle part of the human body. The situation is that this actual I has to do with warmth qualities, just as the physical body has to do with solids, the ether body with fluids and the astral body with gases. The situation is that with everything that relates to his actual I, the human being makes warmth move. This can be seen in detail if we study the human body. The actual I is also connected with the blood, and the blood therefore produces warmth. But the actual I, of which human beings have conscious awareness, is also connected with glandular secretion, for instance. Because of this, glandular secretion is connected with temperature conditions. With its supersensible powers the actual I also uses the powers of the head to prevent fermentation. We are thus able to say: the ether body combats the rotting of proteins, the astral body combats fats going rancid, and the I combats the fermentation of sugar and starch.

This is also the reason why I had to tell you on one occasion[8] that eating too many potatoes is bad for the head. Excessive potato consumption affects the human being as follows. You see, a potato contains little protein, which basically makes it a good human food. And if people eat moderate amounts of potatoes together with other things, the potato is a good food, having little protein. But it contains an extraordinary amount of starch which has to be converted to sugar in the human being, first into dextrin and then into sugar. I told you on that earlier occasion that the head has to do a terrible lot of work when people eat too many potatoes, obviously, for the head has to prevent fermentation. People who eat too many potatoes and have to make a terrible effort in their heads to cope with potato fermentation therefore tend to be weak in the head. It is mainly the middle parts of the brain that grow weak, leaving only the front parts which make little effort to prevent potato fermentation. It is actually due to the fact that potatoes have come to be widely eaten in recent times that materialism has developed, for this is produced in the front part of the brain.

It is really peculiar. People think materialism is a matter of logic. To some extent materialism is nothing but the consequence of eating potatoes! Now I think you'll agree people do not really like it if they have to live mainly on potatoes, but they do like materialism. So they are really caught up in a contradiction. To be a proper materialist, one should really advise everyone to eat potatoes, for that would surely be the best way of being convinced of materialism. But it is something that does not happen with most people. However, if the materialistic monists, the Monist Association, wanted to be really effective in their fight, they should really make sure that other foods are as far as possible replaced with potatoes. Then the Monist Association would be terribly successful. It would not be quick, but over some decades the Monist Association would be most effective if it were to influence the eating of potatoes. Though the people they would seek to influence with their potato diet would also give them something to think about; and so they would not be all that successful.

One thing you can see from this is that the science of the spirit we work with here recognizes the true nature of materialism. Materialism does not know anything about the world of matter; the science of the spirit recognizes the potato in particular as the real creator of materialism. It is dreadfully malicious, the potato, crafty, sly to an excessive degree. For you see, people can only eat the tubers of potatoes, not even the eyes on a potato — they are harmful — and they certainly cannot eat the flowers, for the potato is a member of the deadly nightshade family and the flowers are poisonous. But what is poison? As I told you the last time, large amounts of a poison kill, small amounts, in fine distribution, are medicinal. Potato as such contains much sticky starch, it consists almost entirely of sticky starch. It would be quite unable to live, because the sticky starch would be terribly harmful to it. But it attracts poison from the world at the same time, and destroys the harmful effect that is inside itself. This is why I say it is crafty and sly. It has its poison which removes the effect that would be harmful to it. But the poison in potatoes is particularly harmful to humans; it does not give this ability to them but only the matter which it renders harmless in itself by using the poison. This really is something we may refer to by saying that the potato is a sly, crafty thing. And people must clearly understand that if they eat too many potatoes their midbrain will wither away and it is even possible that their senses also suffer from eating too many potatoes.

If someone eats too many potatoes as a child or a young person, his midbrain will become extraordinarily weak. But the midbrain is the source of the most important sense organs. In the midbrain lie four rounded eminences called colliculi, the thalamus, and so on, and excessive potato consumption even weakens one's eyesight, for this has its origins in the midbrain. Some eye conditions in old age are due to the person having been brought up eating too many potatoes as a child. A person then gets weak eyes, weak eyesight. It really is true that people in Europe suffered much less from weak eyesight in earlier times than they do now. And this is because apart from other things that influence the eyes (but less strongly, because they do not act from inside, electric light and so on) excessive potato consumption in particular is very harmful to the eyes, affecting our vision and even the ability to taste — even the ability to taste! You see, the consequence is as follows. Let us assume someone eats too many potatoes even as a child. Later in life you will very often find that such a person never knows when he has had enough, because his sense of taste has been ruined by potato consumption, while someone who has not eaten too many potatoes will know instinctively when he has had enough. This instinct, which is largely connected with the midbrain, is thus ruined by excessive potato consumption. This is something that has emerged particularly clearly in recent times.

From everything I have said you will see that people must take particular care to be strong enough to overcome firstly the rotting of proteins, secondly the getting rancid of fats, thirdly the fermentation of starch and sugar.

As I told you the last time, people cannot be complete anti-alcoholics — for if they do not take any alcohol at all, alcohol is produced inside them. This alcohol stays in the lower body; it does not go up to the head, for the head must be free from alcohol, otherwise it will be unable, as bearer of the I, to have proper control of the fermentation in the body. You see, you can now have an idea of the way in which human beings relate to their natural environment. Looking at rotting protein everywhere — animals rot away, plants rot away — you have to say: ether is also present everywhere, and this gradually balances it out again. Looking at fats, which are also found in plants, which are found everywhere, you have to say: these fats would gradually make it impossible for all living creatures to continue to live, both animals and humans, if the astral body were not present to combat the process of going rancid. The human being thus fights everything that exists in nature outside. And when the human being dies the ether body, astral body and I go away. They leave the physical body. The human being then moves on into the world of the spirit. What happens then? Well, gentlemen, you know what happens. The dead body immediately begins to rot, to go rancid and at the same time to ferment, though the rotting is more apparent to the eye and to the nose, for we only rarely go about with our noses blocked up. The rotting process is thus easily smelt. But to go and lie across a grave somewhere and taste if the fat of the dead body has gone rancid — that is something we do not normally do, and therefore people usually do not know about it. And the fermentation that takes place is not studied at all. So it truly is the case that because the I goes away the human body begins to ferment, because the astral body goes away the human body goes rancid, and because the ether body goes away the human body starts to rot. This is something human beings always have in them, but for as long as they live on earth they are always fighting it. Anyone who denies that the ether body, the astral body and the I are present in the body as real spiritual entities simply has to be asked: What do you imagine? Why does the human being not rot away? Why does he not ferment? Why does he not go rancid? This would have to happen to the body if it were just a physical body.

What do our scientists do? They wait until a human being has died before they examine him. For they know precious little of the living human being compared to what they know of the anatomy of the dead body, when the human being has died. Everything you are able to learn from them really only relates to the dead body. Scientists always wait for the dead body. They are thus quite unable to know anything about the real human being, who is alive, for they do not consider him. And this is the great problem, that all the knowledge of our modern science – this really is only so since the seventeenth century – basically comes only from the dead body. But the dead body is no longer the human being, for we have to ask ourselves: what brings it about that the dead body which human beings have also when they are alive does not behave like the dead body, rotting, fermenting and going rancid? It is exactly when we take a real look at the living human being that we discover these supersensible aspects of human nature. And we then also find that the I is active mainly in the head, that the astral body is active mainly in the chest, and that the ether body is active mainly in the lower body. And scientists do not know anything about the lower body, for they believe the processes in there are the same as those in outside nature. But that is not so.

Well, gentlemen, it is interesting to study things by not shutting oneself away in one's study but going out among living people. You know there are spas where you get a smell of rotten eggs, in Marienbad[9] for instance, because the water contains hydrogen sulphide. Yes, really, people who like fine foods and are also fussy about smells have to go to such spas. And why do they go? Why do they sometimes spend several summer months in places where it smells as if there were rotten eggs everywhere? You see, it is like this. These people really have eaten too much protein and now come to the spa. They are covered with skin and the whole business is inside, and so they do not smell like that. But if we were able to smell it, they would smell horribly of rotten eggs inside. So all the people who inwardly smell of rotten eggs come to the spas where you get a smell of rotten eggs. And what happens? Well, you see, in one case the rotten egg smell is inside, and in the other it is outside. In the one case, where it is inside, the nose does not notice it; in the other case, where it is outside, the nose does notice. Head and belly are opposites. The rotten egg smell produced in the belly is combated when it comes from the head side, through the sense of smell. And the inner smell of rotten eggs is fought in spas that smell of rotten eggs.

This is very noticeable for anyone who is inclined to make such observations. It so happens that when I was a boy I had to go to such a spa. Every second day I had to go to a spring called Marienquelle.[10] There you also get a smell of rotten eggs. While this is rather unpleasant outwardly, there being such a terrible smell, you suddenly begin to feel rather good in your belly. So if one is not sick, and does not have the rotten egg smell in one's belly, a feeling of greater vitality comes up. Anyone who is not driven away by the smell can experience this. Someone who holds his nose will of course not experience the contrast, will not have this springtime effect in the belly that comes if one really gives oneself up to the rotten egg smell. And rotten egg smell is an extraordinarily good medicine, for example, even if artificially produced. It will give the body the power to make atrophying muscles grow strong and firm again. People are not keen on such treatments, but in one respect they are extraordinarily useful. For you see, if the rotten egg smell comes to us from outside, spring comes inside, in the belly. And in spring everything grows and sprouts, and people can gain new strength when spring comes inside, in their bellies.

This then is what happens with people who ruin their digestion by eating too much during the winter. You see, when someone does not ruin his digestion by eating too much in winter, he shares in the spring that comes in the outside world. The lower body in particular participates in the spring very strongly. But if you want to really enjoy spring in the world of nature outside, you should as far as possible avoid such things as goose liver pâté and so on. If you have eaten a lot of goose liver pâté then the environment in your belly will always be the way it is below the surface of the soil in winter, not above ground but below ground. It is warm there, for it is where pits are dug to store potatoes through the winter. But it all goes rotten in the human being because the warmth is stored in the belly; spring does not come in the human being. And then he must find an artificial spring in the smell of rotten eggs.

This is the contrast between I and ether body. I and ether body must be in balance in the human being. You can see from this that if one really studies things in the world of nature, going to a spa that has the smell of rotten eggs with open senses, the sensation of spring in one's belly teaches one that inwardly the opposite process takes effect as proteins begin to rot.

solid	*physical body*		
fluid	*ether body*	*protein*	*ether body, lower body*
gaseous	*astral body*	*fats*	*astral body, chest*
warmth principle	*I*	*starch, sugar*	*I*

Ether body combats rotting
Astral body combats going rancid
I combats fermentation

I wanted to add to what I said the last time. You know I told you that when someone has taken certain poisons he has to take liquid egg-white protein as an antidote. Things that are healthy become poisons if they are not treated properly in the body, if too much of them gets into the body. Protein can therefore drive away poison in the human being, but protein is itself poisonous if it rots in the body, if too much of it gets into the body. That is how close nutrition and poisoning are to one another. You have no doubt heard that excess food can become poison. A great many diseases are nutritional diseases, that is, people failed to consider that only certain amounts of some substances should be taken if the body is to cope with them.

I'll ask them to tell you when the next talk will be, because I won't be here on Saturday. I'll be in Bern then.

4. Discussion of 2 February 1924

The human eye. Albinism

Gentlemen, the question that has been asked is:
Is the iris of the eye a mirror of soul life in sickness and in health?
I think the second question can be combined with it; they
are probably meant to go together:
How does albinism or leukopathy develop in black people?
To answer this question we must above all consider the
nature of the human eye in some detail. The question has to
do with the fact that some people draw conclusions as to the
sickness or health of the whole body from the state of the
iris, the coloured ring-shaped structure surrounding the
blackness of the pupil in the eye. The iris does indeed show
the greatest imaginable variation in different people. As
you know, it is not merely that it is blue or black or brown or
grey or indeed hazel, but it also has lines created by tiny
vessels that run in different patterns. It is true, therefore,
that just as the general facial features differ from person to
person, so the more subtle structures of this iris or rainbow
membrane differ greatly between people, much more so
than the facial features differ from person to person.

We'll need to go into the structure of the eye to some
extent if we want to talk about the subject. This also relates
to the other question you have asked. It is that especially in
negroes but also in others who are not black, the skin shows
abnormal, unusual colouring and this is connected with the
special colouring of the iris. It is in a way connected. The
skin colouring is particularly striking in black people for the
very reason that the rest of their skin is black, and they then
have all kinds of white spots, looking mottled like a tiger.
They are only rarely completely pale and completely white;

that is extremely rare among negroes, extraordinarily rare. But 'albinos', as they are called, may also be seen in races that are not completely black in colour. Albinism also occurs among white people; they have a very pale skin, an almost milky white. The iris is usually a pale reddish colour, with the pupil, which is black in other people, a dark red. A female albino I once saw was showing herself in all kinds of fair booths. The skin was milky white all over, the iris red, with dark red rather than black pupils, and she said in an uncommonly weak voice: 'I am entirely white, have red eyes and have very poor vision.' And that was true, she could not see well.[11]

If we want to go into the matter we must first of all study the structure of the eye itself. I have been telling you various things in the course of time, and so you will probably be able to understand what I am going to say today. You see, the eye lies in the extremely solid bony part of the head. The bony form of the head arches in there (Fig. 6) and the eye lies in this bony cavity, which is opening towards the brain here at the back. The outer border of the eye to the outside is a hard membrane, which is not transparent here. The eye-

Fig. 6

ball, as it is called, is enclosed in a firm membrane, the external tunic. This becomes transparent at the front, here, where it bulges a little. We would not be able to reach the light with the inner part of the eye if that part of the membrane were not transparent. It is called the cornea in its transparent part because it is hornlike. Next to it to the inside is a membrane consisting of fine blood vessels. The body's blood network extends to the eye, sending extremely fine capillaries into the eye. So we have here the external tunic, which is transparent at the front, and lying close to it the choroid, as it is called. The third membrane inside is made of nerves; it is called the retina. So I have to draw in a third membrane, the retina. This extends backwards, as does the choroid. And this, being nerve substance, going in the direction of vision, is called the optic nerve. You know how people say that we sense things through the nerves. And with the optic nerve we see.

The strange thing is, however, and everyone has to admit this, that we see with the optic nerve in all these parts, but not in the place where it enters; there it is blind and one sees nothing! If someone were to look in such a way that he would be looking just there, somehow, or if the nerves all around were to be diseased and only the place where the optic nerve comes it was healthy, one would nevertheless see nothing at the place where it comes in. Now people say: 'We see with the optic nerve; it is there so that we may see.' Have you ever heard the following? Imagine a group of, say, 30 workers; 25 of them must work busily. They stand all around there. And then there is a group of 5 — it is not the kind of thing one does, but let us suppose it is done like that — and these 5 are allowed to be idle while the others are working hard. So we may say these are the 25 busy workers and there we have 5 who are idle all the time, sitting in comfortable armchairs and doing nothing. If someone were to tell you that the work is just as much done by the 5 idlers—or perhaps he cannot say this, because he does not see it, but the work is done by people being idle—you would not believe him, would you? It is clearly nonsense. But scientists tell us: 'The optic nerve sees.' Yet in the very place where there is most of this nerve it does not see at all! That is just as if you were to say the work is being done by the 5 idlers. You see people actually know these things— that is what is so odd about it—but they will insist on their common or garden nonsense. I think you'll agree that the existence of the blind spot, for that is what it is called, here where the optic nerve comes in most strongly (Fig. 6) and the fact that we do not see anything whatsoever in this spot shows quite clearly that the optic nerve cannot be something we see with.

The matter is like this. There is something in the human body that is very similar to this business with the optic nerve; and that is your two arms and hands. Imagine you pick up a chair. You make a great effort with your arms, including your hands. But the element that connects them remains up here, does it not? It is the same with the optic nerve. You endeavour to do something that reaches out to the light, and in the middle it is just the way it is between the two areas where your arms attach here. But it is not the optic nerve which reaches out—if it were the optic nerve it would have to see most exactly in that spot—but what reaches out is part of the entirely invisible element that I have described to you. This in fact is indeed the I, the I-organization. It is not the physical body, nor the ether body, not even the astral body; it is the I. And so I have to draw in something else, apart from what is already in there: it is the invisible I which spreads there. Except that it is not as if there were two such arms but as if the two arms were to come together and make a sphere. We create part of a sphere when we touch something with our hands. That is how the supersensible I is in there; it takes hold there. And what purpose does the nerve have? Well, gentlemen, the nerve is there—this being work done by the invisible human being—so that secretion may happen. Matter is secreted everywhere and remains lying everywhere. We see with our supersensible I. But the nerve is there so that something may be secreted.

Consider the nonsense scientists talk. It is as if one were to examine the colon and whatever is inside the colon and one would actually say that human beings take their nourishment from the material excreted from the colon! Just as you have matter in the colon which is then excreted, so nerve matter is excreted here. And this (the blind spot) is the place where most of it is excreted. Material not needed in the eye is excreted into the brain and then goes further and is eliminated altogether. You see, this is something you can understand quite easily, yet people tell the weirdest tales about it today. It is simply that people do not realize what it means when others insist that we see with our nerve substance or have sentience or perceive something or other. That would be the same as if we were to take our nourishment from the contents of the colon. So you see that this matter of the blind spot has no significance for the ability to see, for the optic nerve around it does not see either; it is merely that here, where the blind spot is, most matter is excreted. And just as nutrition comes to an end in the colon, and this exists only for the purpose of elimination, so does vision come to an end here, for this is where most is eliminated, and there also is no point to being able to see there in the middle.

Imagine a stick lying there and you were to try and pick it up with your head! You cannot do it. You have to pick it up with your arm, your hand, with something attached to you at the side. In the same way you cannot see with the nerve. You have to see with something that reaches out.

Now, gentlemen, everything you have there (Fig. 6) ends

here in a kind of muscle. This muscle holds the lens. That is a completely transparent body. Why transparent? So that we may get to the light. And behind this body is a thickish liquid. In front is an even thicker liquid, and in this thickish liquid floats the iris, which lies here, close to the blood vessels. It really floats in the liquid, leaving a hole for the light. This hole looks black when you look into it, because you are looking right through the whole eye to the back of this, which is black.

The iris is fairly transparent in front and black at the back. The black membrane at the back is fairly thin in some people. Some people have blue eyes because one is looking through something transparent into blackness when it is thin. And the eyes are black or dark in people who have a thicker membrane, where you are looking at a thick skin at the back of the iris. We'll talk about brown eyes shortly.

We have to consider why it is so, gentlemen, that this membrane, which really is responsible for the blue or brown or black, is thicker or thinner in some people. I have told you that there, into the eye, goes what we call the I, this most sublime supersensible part of the human being. There the I enters. The I is strong or weak to a different degree in people. Take it that the I is very strong in a person, that a person has a very strong I. You see, such a person is able to dissolve the iron he has in his blood — through this choroid membrane it also gets into the eye — completely. Someone who has a strong I thus dissolves the iron completely, and the result is that very little iron gets into this membrane, which after all is in the outermost margin of the body, because it has been completely dissolved. Little iron gets into it, and the result is that this membrane becomes thin-nish. And because it becomes thinnish, one has blue eyes. Now imagine someone has a weak I; he then does not dissolve the iron so much, and the result will be that a great deal of undissolved iron still gets into this membrane. This undissolved iron makes the membrane thicker, and a person has dark, black eyes. It thus depends on the I whether a person has black or blue eyes.

Well, gentlemen, there is also another substance in the blood, and that is sulphur. Even if the I is able to deal with the iron, it is sometimes unable to deal with the sulphur. When the I lets undigested sulphur enter into this membrane, a yellowy brown develops in the iris, and a person has brownish eyes. If especially large amounts of sulphur get into the eyes, the iris will be reddish. Even the pupil is not black in that case, because of the sulphur that shimmers behind it. That is the case with albinos, with people who also cannot properly provide their skin with colour. We may say, therefore, that there are people who can inject sulphur into their eyes, as it were. The I can inject it, and this produces the unusual colouring of the iris.

But anything that gets into the eye by way of sulphur or iron also gets into the whole body, for it comes from the blood. Those are just tiny blood vessels here in the eye. If someone injects sulphur here in the eye, he also injects sulphur into the whole of his skin everywhere. And the result of thus injecting sulphur everywhere into the skin is that he does not have the natural skin colouring in these places where the sulphur has been injected; for our natural skin colour comes from iron being processed. If someone therefore only processes his iron slightly and injects sulphur instead, he gets those patchy skin areas and one can at the same time also see it in the eyes.

So you see, it is exactly when we consider this invisible human being who is present in every person that we can understand the human being right down to the level of physical matter. Anthroposophy is not so idiotic that one cannot understand matter. It is the materialists who actually do not understand matter. If you read about albinism anywhere — what do your read? The one among you who has asked the question will probably have read somewhere that the cause of albinism is unknown. Materialists arrive at this strange statement that the cause is unknown because they pay no heed at all to the situations where the causes are to be found. It is of course easy to say: That is a red pupil. Yes, but one must know what is really at work in there, and what is injecting the business, for both the red and the pale colouring of the body come from the sulphur.

Now you'll be able to understand the nature of true science. Imagine you go somewhere on earth where some work has been done. Someone looks at it and says: 'The work is there, the cause is unknown.' He does not care about what happened before. He therefore says: 'Cause unknown.' The fact that 30 people have been working there for many days, for example, does not concern him. That is what scientists do when they say the cause of the red hue of the pupil and the pale hue of the skin is unknown. But the cause lies in the I which is at work there in the physical matter.

You also see from this that the iris does indeed have something of a true mirror image of the way the whole body works with iron and sulphur. But just take such an albino. That is really a kind of illness. Too much work is done with sulphur in the body, but the body gets used to it and things are organized that way. Now it may happen that the degree to which this gets into the eyes is much less. You see, apart from the albino lady who was showing herself in a fair booth, I have seen quite a few other albinos. And it is always possible to show that there is a very special situation with such albinos. You may say: 'There's an albino, and he has this unusual red colouring of the iris, a pale red, with the pupil dark red, and has a pale body.' If you now examine him further you come to see, from the nature of his body, that the connection between heart and kidney is particularly weak. The kidneys are only supplied with blood with great difficulty and therefore only function laboriously. If this person were to deposit the sulphur which he has in him because of the nature of this whole body in the kidneys, he would die in childhood. He therefore gets rid of the sulphur by pushing it into the body surface — the skin gets white, the eyes are red — so that the kidneys can work delicately. Those albinos have the most delicately functioning kidneys, for instance. The same may happen in other people. But when people who are not albinos — most of them are not albinos — develop any kind of kidney defect, surely this must also show itself in the iris? For anything sulphur and iron do with one another is also reflected here. And so it is possible to see from this subtle reflection in the iris if there is a spot here or here that is not really normal: there you have damage in the body. But you have to consider, gentlemen, that the human body is a whole, and if one were clever enough to do this one could also see what is seen in the iris if one cut out a little bit of skin. Then something abnormal would also show itself in the skin, or in the nail of the big toe if one were to cut it off. There, too, you have very subtle distinctions, and you would be able to see from this that the liver or the kidney or the lung are not all right, though it would be a little bit different again. But if someone were particularly clever and examined cut-off fingernails rather than the iris, for example — it would be much harder because it is less obvious — he would also be able to see if the body is healthy or sick. It is noticeable in the eye simply because the eye is a particularly delicate structure, and subtle changes are easily perceived there. But you can see in other ways, too, that things emerge most strongly on the body surface. I have rarely seen someone wanting to get the feel of a very fine fabric or something like that put it on his shoulders. If this were to be the better method, we would of course arrange things in such a way that if we wanted to get the feel of something very fine we would bare the area up on the shoulder and touch and feel it there. But that does not get us anywhere. We feel it with our fingertips. And in the fingertips we are particularly sensitive to get the feel of things. So there we have the same again as before. If it were the nervous system that really allowed us to feel things, we ought to feel things most up there, close to the brain. But we do not have the strongest sense of touch close to the brain but furthest away from it, in the outermost fingertips, because the I is most of all located on the body surface. It is easiest to see what someone is inwardly, as an I, from the outermost surface. And because the eyes are most of all on the surface, this is also where one is most able to see these things, because the eyes are delicate and away from the brain.

You may say the eyes are in the skull and close to the brain. But we have many bones there to make sure they are really far away, and at the point where the eye connects with the brain, where there is no bone, nothing is seen at all. In the case of the fingertips it is therefore due to the distance in space that they are particularly sensitive; in the case of the eyes it is because they are most strongly shielded from the brain.

Something else is also strange. When a lower animal develops its brain, it does so in such a way that the brain leaves a cavity for the eye, and the eye does not grow out of the brain but becomes attached to the side there and grows into the cavity. The eye grows from the outside, not out of the brain; it grows into the brain. Is is therefore produced from outside.

You can see from all this that whatever is produced on the surface, be it in the skin, be it in the eye, has to do with something that most closely connects the human being with the outside world. If someone always stays in bed, unable to use his will for the body, we cannot really say that he strongly develops his I. If someone is very mobile, we can indeed say that he brings his I strongly to expression. And it is the senses that apart from this keep us in touch with the outside world—in our smelling, seeing and so on. And the eye is the most delicate of senses to keep us in touch with the outside world. So we may well say that because the I is particularly active in this fine network of capillaries (those are terribly fine vessels in the iris) we can see a great deal from it—how the whole I works in an inward direction, that is, if a person is healthy or sick.

This is the first truth and insight we have relating to this matter. But this fact which I have been describing to you is also one of the most difficult, for one has to be extremely well informed as to what a minor irregularity in the iris may signify if one is to draw conclusions about a person being healthy or sick. Let me give you an example. You see, it may be, for example, that small dark dots appear here and there in someone's iris. These dark dots mean, of course, that the person has something which is not there if there are no dark dots in the iris. But let us assume this person, in whom the dark dots appear, is a terribly stupid fellow. He will then have some kind of illness that is indicated by those dots. But it may also be that the person who has those dark dots had excessive demands made on him in his youth to learn things, and this learning process went beyond his physical powers. The fact that he used certain organs too much in his youth may have driven a certain weaker activity into his eyes, and it may then happen that these small, fine iron deposits appeared due to overexertion in his childhood. They may thus appear due to illness in later life, but they may also appear due to overexertion in childhood. Most people tend to think: if I see little black dots in the iris then one thing or another must be the case in the body. It is, however, important to know not only about the person's present life. Particularly if one wants to look at such things in order to discover the causes of illness one must go through such a person's whole life with him; one must make him remember what he did on one occasion or another in his childhood. What we see in the iris may thus point to a number of things. And it requires extremely complex knowledge to draw any conclusions from this.

This is why it is so annoying when people write all kinds of pamphlets today. The things they write are usually quite brief, under the title of 'eye diagnosis'. You get 50 pages of instructions on how the iris should be examined. Like this, you see: there is the divided-up iris, there is the pupil, a completely schematic representation. Then it says 'disease of the spleen'; 'lung disease', 'syphilis' and so on. An eye diagnostician who knows what can be seen when he looks at the iris through a medium magnifying glass then only needs to refer to his booklet. And when he sees markings in the area where it says lung disease, he will say: 'lung disease'! And that is what many eye diagnosticians do today, after just an hour's study. They leave the rest to the booklet they have; they just make the diagnosis. Gentlemen, that is disgusting! You have something extremely difficult and these people want to learn it in the easiest possible way. The result is not something of value but quite the opposite. Damage is done to the whole field of medicine. And people must make the distinction between someone who has serious intentions in medicine or merely wants to make money.

People are of course upset about science today, rightly so, for if you take the example of the optic nerve I have given you, scientists pay no heed to what the human being really is but appreciate the excrement above all else in the human being, that excrement in the eye, for example, that is the optic nerve. People do not know this, of course, but they feel it, and get annoyed with scientists. One can understand their annoyance. But what eye diagnosticians generally do is not better than science but generally much worse. Out of ignorance, knowing no better because of modern materialism, scientists believe excrement to be the most sublime part of the human being. Excrement is, of course, most necessary, for if it were to remain in the body it would soon kill the body; it is therefore necessary. But scientists consider excrement to be the most valuable thing in the human being. But they are taking a right and proper course, for they do not just want to make money. It is just that they are struck with blindness. They have a very large blind spot in their knowledge; yet in spite of it all we have to acknowledge their good will. But when it comes to those eye diagnosis pamphlets, we cannot speak of good will, only of a desire to make money. So you always have to say to yourself with such things: a good truth may be at the heart of some endeavour, but it is exactly the best truths, gentlemen, that are most abused by the world. You see, it is truly marvellous that the whole human being in health and sickness is indeed reflected in the iris. But on the other hand the iris is hardest to diagnose for its own condition just because the whole human being is reflected in it in health and sickness, and we really have to say that anyone who does eye diagnosis without real knowledge of the whole human being is doing mischief.

What does it mean, to know the whole human being? You see, we have learned that the human being consists of his physical body, the ether body, the astral body and the I. One therefore not only has to know something of the physical body but must also know something of the spiritual human being, especially if one wishes to do eye diagnosis. You know, ordinary anatomy, which is only concerned with the dead body, may sometimes be adequate in what it has to offer; it may still offer something quite good, relatively speaking. Anatomists may not know that the optic nerve is the excrement of the eye, but they do at least find the optic nerve. But an eye diagnostician usually has not the least idea of how the nerve runs. He has his 50-page booklet showing divisions of the iris and diagnoses away; he does not examine the person. Then he'll of course need some other booklet, again of 50 pages. There the rubric 'lung disease' may be found and the remedy for it. But lung disease is something that may be from many causes. Knowing that the lung is affected does not tell us much. The lung affection may come from the digestion. One needs to know where it comes from. Many people have lung disease. In many of them the lung disease has a wide variety of causes. This is exactly where one has to be tremendously careful, for where you get the best things you also have the greatest mischief done. I told you often in these lectures that the human being depends not only on the earth but on the whole of the starry heavens. But that is exactly also what calls for the most complex insight. And one should not cause mischief here. Fraud and mischief are practised on a large scale by the different astrologers in the world today. It is much the same with eye diagnosis as it is in astrology. In astrology, one also has something sublime and magnificent. But there is nothing very sublime about the people who do astrology today. In most cases designs on other people's purses are the basis of their work.

And so you can see the connection, gentlemen. On the one hand we have phenomena that change the whole surface of a person, even externally. The person develops pale skin areas, the rest of the skin being darker, his eyes get a different colour; he is an albino. A certain activity is driven to the surface, deflected from the internal organs. But when someone is not an albino, the same things, the external appearance of the eye, are present in the iris, but the finer structure, the finer differentiation points to the inner organism. An albino is not totally ill from being an albino, he merely has the disposition for a disease because he has this from his young days and his bodily organization later gets used to it.

You see it is not good to call an albino a leukopath. It suggests that the blood of such people is different, leukocytes being particular corpuscles in the blood. The cause is not known. But when the blood grows paler on the surface, you do not get general green-sickness or anaemia, but the skin gets paler on the surface. That is the difference between the disease of green-sickness, where the blood inside simply gets paler, and leukopathy or albinism, where the blood is more pushed towards the surface. The situation is that when someone has anaemia, an internal function is out of order. The I is more active on the surface, the astral body more inside. Because of this, all the bodies we see or hear with are pushed more to the surface. We need those for the I. The liver we need inside. And if you were to feel everything your liver does as strongly as that, you would be observing your innards all the time, saying: 'Ah, I've just got some cabbage soup into my stomach, the walls of the stomach are beginning to absorb it. It is as though it radiates out, very interesting. Now it goes through the pylorus at the end of the stomach into the duodenum; it now reaches the villi in the intestinal walls.' You would take note of all this, and all of it would be most interesting, but you would have no time at all to take note of the outside world! It is very interesting and there is lots to observe, in many respects much more beautiful than the outside world, but human beings are quite rightly distracted from this. Generally speaking it does not come to conscious awareness; the things that are on the surface come to conscious awareness. If someone therefore does not digest the iron properly inside, where the astral human being is more active, he gets anaemic. If he does not properly deal with the iron outside, but dissolves it, as I have described it to you, he becomes an albino — which is very rare; he gets leukopathy.

So you see that the question I have been asked has to do with this: albinism is due to the I not digesting sulphur or iron in a regular way. Anaemia comes from abnormal iron processing by the astral body and affects more the inner part of the blood. And if one really understands what goes on inside the human being one can also see which super-sensible aspect of the human being is involved. Someone with proper understanding of the physical human being also understands the super-physical, supersensible human being. But the situation with materialism is this: materialists do not understand the supersensible human being and therefore also do not understand the physical human being.

I'll have them tell you if I'll be back next Wednesday. Maybe someone will have another question for the next session, so that we may have a similar discussion based on that question.

Fluid cycle of earth in relation to universe

Today, gentlemen, I'd like to say a few more things that may help to explain some of the things we have already been discussing, and then you may prepare the questions that come to you for the next time. Today I'd like to talk about some things that may make you aware again how the earth — which as you know is a spherical body in the universe — relates to the whole world. Let us study this today by considering rivers and oceans.

You know that the earth only partly shows solid land on its outside; it is mainly a sphere of water that moves within the universe, a watery sphere, an ocean. And in general terms we may say that rivers have their origin somewhere on earth, their source, and run to the sea. Let us take the Danube, for example. You know the Danube has its source in the Black Forest. Or take the Rhine. You know it originates in the southern Alps. The Danube then flows through various valleys until it reaches the Black Sea. The Rhine flows through various valleys into the North Sea. Now, we generally consider only the course a river takes and how it runs into the sea. We take delight in rivers. We do not consider the tremendous significance which rivers and the sea really have for the whole of life on earth.

With a human being we are usually able to say more about what is liquid in him. As I have told you, the human being is largely also a mass of fluid. And you know that in a certain type of fluidity the blood flows in his veins. We also know that the fact that the blood flows has the greatest imaginable importance for life. Blood creates life, sustains life. As physical human beings we are totally dependent on

the blood flowing through the body in the right way, following particular pathways. If it were to go astray from
those pathways, we would not be able to live. People do not
usually realize that the way the waters are arranged in
rivers and oceans has equally great importance for the
earth. People do not usually realize that water really makes
up the earth's blood circulation. Why do people fail to
realize this?

You see, with the blood we cannot fail to notice; it is red, it
contains all kinds of substances, and so we say to ourselves:
The blood is something special. With water, we simply
think: Ah well, it's water. It attracts less notice; and the
substances it contains – apart from hydrogen and oxygen,
which are in water – are not present in such large quantities
as iron is, for instance, in the blood. So people pay no heed
to this. But it is true, nevertheless, that the whole water
circulation has tremendous significance for the life of the
earth. And just as the human organism could not live if it
did not have its blood circulation, so would the earth be
unable to live if it did not have its water circulation.

This water circulation has the special characteristic that at
its beginning it originates in something quite different from
what it ends in when it runs into the sea. You see, if you
follow rivers you find they do not contain salt; the water is
fresh. Rivers contain fresh water. The sea contains salt. And
everything the sea gives rise to is due to its salt content. This
is extraordinarily important: the water begins to circulate as
fresh, salt-free water on earth, and it ends in a salty state in
the sea.

People usually say: 'All right, a river such as the Rhine
has its source somewhere, it flows on (Fig. 7) like this and
then runs into the sea.' This is what one sees on the outside.
But what people fail to note is that the river, the Rhine, for
example, does outwardly flow like that, but while its waters
outwardly flow from the southern Alps to the North Sea, a

Fig. 7

kind of energy current runs below ground from the mouth of the river back to its origin. It goes back. And what happens there (above ground) is that the river has fresh water, with no salt in it. What happens there (underground) always brings salt into the earth, along the river, so that the earth receives salts into itself that really come from the sea. We thus have a salt stream running underground, from the mouth of a river to its origin. And the earth would not have any salt if that salt stream did not run back underground from the mouths of the rivers to their origin. Geologists, who study the inner parts of the earth, will therefore always have to pay attention to the salt deposits that are to be found some way down wherever there are river beds.

You see, gentlemen, if there were no salt deposits in the soil, plants roots could not grow in it, for plant roots grow in the soil exactly only because they have the salt of the earth, as it were, for their food. Plants have the highest salt content down in the root; above ground they contain less and less salt, with only a little in the flowers. We may thus ask: why is it that our soil can produce plants? It is merely because it has a water circulation, that just as in us humans arteries go out from the heart and veins go back to it carrying the blue blood, so the arteries of the waters go in one direction on the earth's surface and salt veins go back. So that you also have a real circulation there.

Why is it, anyway, that the earth on the one hand consists of a watery salt body, and on the other of solid land, and then of bodies of fresh water, rivers that flow through the lands, and that salt is continually brought in from the seas in such a way? Well, you see, if you examine the actual salt water, sea water that contains a lot of salt, you find that this salty sea water has little connection with universal space. Just as our stomachs, for instance, have little connection with the outside world, except for what comes into them, so does the inner aspect of the sea have little connection with the heavens. But all lands where rivers flow, where plants are produced because there are salt deposits, but above all where waters flow, are very much connected with the heavens.

Looking at the matter like this, gentlemen, we go to our mountain springs in a very different mood. We delight in the trickling, flowing springs with their wonderfully clear water, and so on. But that is not all. The springs are the earth's eyes. The earth does not look out into cosmic space with the ocean, for the sea is salty and that means that inwardly it is only the way our stomach is inwardly. The springs that flow with fresh water are open to the cosmos and are like our eyes, which also open to the outside world. We may thus say that on land, where you have springs, the earth looks out far into cosmic space, there you have the earth's sense organs, whereas the body of the earth, or rather the innards of the earth, are the salty oceans. It is of course different from the way it is in the human body; these are not organs complete in themselves, organs you can draw in their entirety. You could draw them but they are not entirely visible. But the earth has its innards in the ocean and its sense organs in the lands. And everything that connects the earth with cosmic space comes from fresh water. Everything that gives the earth its innards comes from salt water.

I am going to prove to you that this is so. You see, I once told you that human and animal reproduction are connected with the heavens. I told you that this is not only because the egg, the embryo in the mother's body develops only in this maternal body but also because influences are coming from the universe, and it is exactly because of these influences from the cosmos that the egg develops its roundness. As we look out and around and see the movement in the universe, so this small egg is an image of the universe, for these influences come from all sides. It means that heaven is active on earth wherever reproduction is active. In the same way you see that the eye is a sphere. I described it the other day. It has also been created under the influence of the universe. If you look at the spleen, it is not spherical but more created by the earth, by earthly influences. And that is the difference. Such things give us proof if we take note of them. I said I would give you proof of the true nature of sea and land.

Here I'd like to bring in something else. As I have told you, we did experiments to establish the role of the spleen in our biology laboratory. The role of the spleen is that when we are unable to eat at regular intervals it serves to balance this out again; it is the regulator. We have provided proof of this in our biological laboratory. It is all described in a small book by Mrs Kolisko.[12] It also became necessary with those experiments — because modern science demands this — to give proof, tangible evidence. This will no longer be necessary when scientists believe in supersensible evidence, but today it is still necessary. We took a rabbit—not causing the rabbit pain in any other way, one can do this with great care—removed the spleen and let the creature live on. This went very well. The rabbit would not have died of the spleen operation but it accidentally caught a cold and perished from that. We then dissected it and were of course most interested to see what had happened where the spleen had been removed. What do we have to say in the light of spiritual science? What remains when the physical spleen is cut out? Well, you see, if this is the spleen (Fig. 8) and you cut it out and put it away, the ether body of the spleen still remains in the site and so does the astral body and so on. The spleen develops under the influence of the earth, and this gives it its shape. If we now remove the physical spleen and only the etheric spleen is in there, as in our rabbit, what has to happen? Well, gentlemen, the following has to happen. While the physical spleen depends on the earth, inclines to the earth, the etheric spleen, which has become completely free, being no longer weighed down by the physical spleen, must again come under the influence of the heavens. And one has to assume that something like an image of heaven would have to develop. And lo and behold, when we dissected the rabbit, we found a small round body inside, made up of fine white tissue! So it all fitted. What has to happen according to the postulates of spiritual science

Fig. 8

did happen. A small nut-sized tissue body had developed in a relatively short time. So you see, we only have to find the right approach and we will everywhere find proof of what spiritual science has to tell us. You can see from this that things we are able to establish on the basis of the science of the spirit, finding the right way of following the issue, do indeed happen in the physical world.

And just as this white body developed under the influence of the surrounding world, so does the human embryo, the animal embryo, initially develop as a sphere in the egg under the influence of the heavens.

Knowing this we have to say that fish are a special case, for they do not really ever come on land. They can at most gasp a little on land, but they cannot live on land, they have to live in the sea. Because of this fish have their own special arrangements. They do not reach the places where the earth opens up to cosmic events. Fish therefore find it very difficult to develop their senses and especially their reproductive organs. For it is due to cosmic space that these can be internal. Fish must therefore carefully utilize the little light and warmth that enters into the sea from the universe if they are to be able to reproduce and to have sense organs. But nature takes care of many things. You can see it in the little goldfish. They use the whole of their skin to come under the influence of the light. This is what makes them golden. Fish use every opportunity to snap up anything that drops into the water from the universe. And they must always deposit their eggs in places where some light still gets in, so that these eggs are given brood care from outside. Fish are thus equipped, as it were, to live under water; they do not leave the water. But what I am saying concerns not so much fresh water fish—fresh water is open to the universe—but sea fish. Sea fish always show that they are ready to utilize everything that still reaches the salt water from the universe to enable them to reproduce.

Salmon are a strange exception, however. They have a special organization. Salmon must live in the sea to develop proper muscles. They need earth influences to feed properly and develop muscles. Those earth influences are mainly in the salt in the sea. Salmon must live in the salt of the sea in order to develop strong muscles. But they cannot reproduce if they live in the sea, because they are made in such a way that the sea water closes them off completely from the universe. Salmon would have died out long ago if they had had to reproduce in the sea. They are the exception. As they gain their strength in the sea — where they develop their muscle — they are in the first place fairly blind, and in the second place are unable to reproduce. Their reproductive organs and their sense organs grow weak, they are dull. But salmon grow big in the sea. Now to prevent the salmon from dying out — we can see this by considering the salmon in the North Sea and over in the Atlantic — salmon migrate up the Rhine year after year. This is why they are called Rhine salmon. But the Rhine makes salmon lean; they lose their muscles. The size to which they have grown in the salty sea is lost in the Rhine. The salmon get really slender; they lose their muscles. Their sense organs and above all their reproductive organs, male and female, develop to an enormous degree, and the salmon are able to reproduce in the Rhine. The salmon must thus migrate from the salty sea to the freshwater Rhine every year in order to reproduce. They have to grow lean, because fresh water cannot help their muscle development. Then, the old ones who are still living and the young ones that have arrived all migrate back to the sea, to lose their slenderness and gain in size.

You see, gentlemen, it fits perfectly. We may say that where the earth is salty it acts with earth forces. It acts on the organs that have been developed out of earth principles. Our own muscles are developed out of earth principles when we move in the field of gravity. Gravity is the earth principle. The earth influences everything that is muscular, and everything that is bony. The earth gives us its salt and we get strong bones, strong muscles. But we can do nothing for our sense and reproductive organs with this salt coming from the earth. They would wither in the process. They must always come under the influence of forces from beyond this earth, influences from heaven. And the salmon show this, making a distinction between salt and fresh water. They go into salt water to fatten up, taking in earth influences, and into fresh water to be able to reproduce, taking in heavenly influences.

We are thus able to say that the earth has a kind of circulation also when it comes to animals, like the salmon for instance. Salmon feel driven to move to and fro between the sea and the river. They go to and fro, to and fro. The whole salmon company goes to and fro. Looking at salmon we can really see how all of life is in motion on earth.

Seeing this as we study salmon, we also gain a picture of something else, a marvellous spectacle that is always in front of our eyes—the migration of birds. They merely move to and fro in the air; salmon move to and fro in water. The migration of salmon in water is just like the migration of birds in the air, except that salmon move to and fro between salt water and fresh water, and the birds in the air move to and fro between the colder and warmer regions they need. If you understand the migration of salmon you also have an idea of the migration of birds. It all has to do with the fact that birds must also go south in order to find the right temperature conditions on earth; there they, too, develop muscle. They need to go to the purer air of the North to have the influences that come from the heavens; there they develop their reproductive organs. These animals need the whole earth. Only the mammals, being higher animals, and human beings have become more independent of the earth, have emancipated more from the earth, getting more independent in their whole organization.

But it only seems like that. You see, we human beings are really always two people. We are actually more than that, as I have told you—physical human being, etheric human being, and so on. But even as physical human beings we are really two people—one on the right and one on the left. The right side of the body differs enormously from the left. I think very few of you, who are sitting here in front of me, will be able to write with the left hand; we write with the right. But the part which is connected with speech, for instance, in the nervous system is located in the left side of the brain. There you have marked convolutions, but not in the matching area on the right. It is the opposite for left-handed people. Left-handed individuals have their speech organization on the right—this is not the outer aspect of speech but the inner one, which stimulates speech. You see, gentlemen, we are able to say that people are enormously different on the left side and the right. And it is the same in other places. The heart is more to the left, the stomach to the left, the liver to the right. Even organs that are on the whole symmetrical are not entirely so. The lung has two lobes on the left and three on the right. The right thus differs greatly from the left in human beings. Why is that so? Well, let us start with something very simple. We do not usually learn to write with the left but with the right hand. This is an activity that depends more on the ether body. The physical body has more weight, is more developed on the left, the ether body is more developed on the right. The left human being develops two lobes; the right, being more active, brings life into the lung, develops three lobes in the lung. The situation is that people are more physical on the left and more etheric on the right. And that is also how it is with speech. Right-handed people need more nutrition in the left side of the brain than in the right side. And all kinds of things in us are arranged in such a way that we contain more of the earth forces on the left and more of the etheric powers of heaven on the right.

You see, gentlemen, our modern science, where only matter is considered, with the result that little is known of the material realm, has led to a bad thing in education, with children made to learn everything equally on the left and on the right. But the human being is not made that way! If one goes too far with this, people are educated to be half crazy, for the body is made to be more physical on the left and more etheric on the right. But what do modern scientists care about physical and etheric! To them, it is all the same, left human being and right human being. We have to be able to penetrate these things with the science of the spirit if we are to understand them at all. On the left, therefore, human beings are more earthly, on the right, we may say, hoping that it will not be misunderstood, more heavenly, more cosmic.

Now human beings have already emancipated a great deal from the earth. As I have told you, they develop this earthly left side and heavenly right side in such a way that they can take it all about with them as physical human beings, and one is really no longer aware that they are inclined to the earth on the left and to heaven on the right. But there are people who are more inclined towards the earth; they mostly tend to sleep on their left side, lying on the left. People will lie on their right side either because they are tired on the left, or because they are more occupied with powers that incline more towards heaven. These things are of course difficult to observe, because all kinds of other things also come into it. After all, a person may simply lie on the left to sleep because that is the dark side of the room; so he also has a reason. It is difficult to observe using our thoughts, or with other things, but generally speaking it will no doubt be the case that someone would tend to lie on the left when going to sleep because that is the earth side. But we really do not need to look at this because human beings have emancipated from the earth and become independent of the earth in their actions. But we may study it in animals.

We see the secrets of the world strangely revealed everywhere. Imagine this is the surface of the sea (Fig. 9), beneath it is the salty sea water with all kinds of other substances in it. Now there are some fish that are organized in a very strange way. These fish are organized in such a way that they are greatly inclined towards the earth forces, while all other fish really snap up everything they can that enters into the water by way of light and air. Having no lungs they cannot breathe when in the air; they die in the air, perish in it, but they snap up anything by way of air and light that gets into the water with their gills. There is one fish, however—large species are called halibut, smaller ones plaice or sole—and they are excellent food, with many nutrients, almost the most nutrients of all fish. This immediately shows that they are inclined towards the earth, for nutrients come from the earth. Our halibut is all for the earth, it is! Now what can we expect from these fish? We can expect that they also show outwardly in their lives that they are for the earth. And they do. They lie so much on one side that it turns pale, white. And they lie so much on that one side that the head turns round and the eyes come to be on the other side. A flatfish therefore looks like this from

Fig. 9

Fig. 10

underneath (Fig. 10). It is quite flat and white. And on the other side, seen from above, the eyes are both on the one side. The head has turned round, because the fish is always lying on the left, as it were. The left side becomes the nutrient side, is pale and white. The other side takes its colour from the sky and so on, turning bluish, brownish, and the eyes actually turn away from the nutrient side, with the head turning round. Such a flatfish is completely one-sided, with its eyes, all organs, on one side; the other side is flat and pale. Halibut really develop many nutrients in them, because they incline to the earth. Some get to more than 300 kilograms [47 stone]. They are big fish, therefore, and widely caught for food. Now these halibut show quite clearly that their body relates to the earth, always lying on the one side. And they lie so much on one side that if a person were to lie on the left every night his head might turn round and he, too, would always look in one direction. But it does not go as far as that with people. Human beings have emancipated from the earth, they keep themselves independent of the earth.

But something may happen also with human beings. It could certainly be that you find a person with a strange disease, for he sees slightly better with the right eye, or one

eye altogether, than with the other. If this is not something
he was born with, and we ask questions, we usually find
that this person lies on the other side to sleep. The earth
forces influence the side one lies on frequently; the eye
grows a bit weaker, has weaker vision. The effect is not as
powerful as in the halibut, but there is a bit of it. The eye
which faces outwards towards the heavens, being turned
away from the earth, grows a little stronger. You see, such
strange connections exist. I told you that somewhere or
other nature will show us the forces it works with. When
you see plaice—this small plaice may be seen in fish mar-
kets everywhere, the large flatfish are in the sea, in salt
water—you say to yourself: all that can develop there is
something that is filled with nutrients; it needs to be dissolved. If these creatures want to have something of heaven,
they must always let the other side face the heavens; then
the eyes move that way, and that way the animals also
become able to reproduce. They use another way than salmon do, therefore. Salmon migrate, moving from the North
Sea into the Rhine, from the Rhine into its tributaries, so that
they may reproduce. Flatfish lie on one side so that the
heavens may influence the other side and they may have
senses and be able to reproduce.

And the earth itself, what does it do? Well, gentlemen, if
we had only salty oceans, the earth would long since have
perished, being unable to maintain itself. It does not only
have salty sea water but also fresh water, and the fresh
water receives powers of procreation from the heavens. The
salty sea cannot draw from cosmic space the element that
always refreshes the earth. If you go to a spring and see the
trickle of marvellously pure water, you will note the lovely
smell of freshness all around it. That freshness around the
spring also refreshes the whole living earth. There the earth
opens up to cosmic space as though through eyes and sense
organs. And we can see from creatures like salmon and

plaice that they go to find it. They have a kind of instinct that makes them cling to the earth element. Salmon go straight to fresh water. Flatfish turn to the light by arranging their bodies in that way. But the springs are like the flatfish; they are the places on earth where the earth turns to the light. The flatfish has to turn directly to the light with its own body.

We can learn such a lot from these things, for they show us things that also exist in human beings, but can no longer be observed so well in human beings because, as I have told you, they have become emancipated from the earth. If one pays no attention to these things one really cannot understand life on earth at all. It is really the case that we may say: looking at the sea and seeing the flatfish we can see the sea opening up to the heavens everywhere through the flatfish. The flatfish are proof that the sea thirsts for the heavens, for its salt content turns it away from the heavens. We may say that flatfish give expression to the sea's thirst for light and air.

Looking at our own circulation, we have subtle sense organs, organs of touch, in the places where we get more salty, where the muscles are. There human beings also open up to the outside—not the way they do in the eyes, where they open up directly to the light. Those are the places, we might say, where the flatfish are in the sea. These flatfish open up to the heavens. And the heavens give them an extraordinary cleverness. Just as we get dextrous from making good use of our outer organs of touch, so do flatfish get dextrous from opening up to the heavens. Down in the sea things are clumsy, awkward—just take a look at them. The flatfish—ah, they get truly dextrous. They become clever creatures because they turn away from the sea on one side. They may indeed turn to the earth forces, saying: the earth forces are kept to themselves, piling up nutrients, up to 47 stone, as I said. But they have these subtle organs through which they open up to heaven. Flatfish eat other fishes, smaller ones. But you see, the fishes would move away on either side when such a flatfish came along, especially because it is like a spectre to them, for the other fishes consider it necessary to have eyes on both sides, to have developed them equally on both sides. Flatfish are to them rather as if a human being were to come towards them. The fishes would move away quickly and the flatfish would have nothing to eat — unless they were cleverer than the others. But the other fishes, those with eyes on both sides, are not so clever because they do not turn so strongly to the heavens. Flatfish settle in places where the sea has a bit of shore, where it is relatively shallow. They push their way into the earth, using their mouths to cover themselves with a bit of sand, and then stir up sand to make a fine veil, fine enough for a fish to swim through. So fishes and crabs come along and do not notice the flatfish, and suddenly, as they move past, the flatfish snaps them up. It does it in an extraordinarily clever way! But this is of course something that can only be done by a creature that finds a subtle way of connecting with the powers of heaven, the powers of the universe.

On the one hand, therefore, such a creature has developed its physical body, and on the other it develops a particularly strong ether body. We can see from such things that everything which we, too, have by way of spiritual powers does not come from the earth forces. The earth forces make us muscular, giving us salts, and the powers of heaven really give us the powers which are then both powers of procreation and powers of mind and spirit, powers that make us clever.

You see, the situation with the human being is that he is basically a small earth globe. Man, too, as I have often told you, consists of 90% of water. And the human being is really also a fish, for the solid human being — floating in the water—makes up only 10%. Basically we are all fishes swimming in our own water. Modern science admits this, that we certainly are in the main a small ocean. And just as the sea sends out rivers, so does our sea, our body of fluids, send out salt-free juices. We, too, have fresh water currents. These are outside our muscles and bones. In our muscles and bones on the other hand we have the same salt deposits as the sea does. There we really have our nutrition, in muscles and bone. We are definitely a small earth globe in this respect, with our salty sea inside us.

If someone develops in such a way that his fluids, his freshwater currents, get too strong—this can easily happen in children, when the milk does not have enough salts in it—he or she gets rickets. Getting too much salt a person becomes too much sea; his bones grow brittle and his muscles clumsy and awkward. There always has to be the right balance between taking in salt and the things to be found in other foods.

What things are there in other foods? Look at a plant, gentlemen. You know plants grow because salty currents go back inwardly where rivers flow down to the sea; they spread and make the plants grow. In the soil, therefore, plants have their salt in there, in their roots (Fig. 11). But when the plant grows out of the soil it grows more and more towards flowering. The flower develops beautiful colours because it takes in light. Out there in the flower, the plant takes in light; in the root it takes in salt. Out there the plant becomes a bearer of light, down there a bearer of salts. Down there it becomes similar to the oceanic part of the earth, up above it becomes similar to the heavens. The root is rich in salts, the flower in light. People knew much more of this in the past. This is why they called the principle to be found in the flower 'phosphorus'. Today, when everything has become material, phosphorus is merely a solid. Phosphorus—*phos* means light, *phor* means bearer. Phosphorus

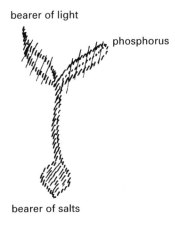

Fig. 11

means bearer of light; phosphorus originally was the principle that bears the light in the flower. The mineral came to
be called phosphorus because if you set fire to it you can see
the light come out. But the flower is the true bearer of light.
The flower is phosphorus. We may say, therefore, that we
need light for the organs in our human body that contain
the freshwater currents, as it were; we need the principle
that plants give us when they move towards the light. For
our muscles, for our bones, for the part of us that should be
salty, we need salt and the solid parts in our foods. And the
balance between them must be right. The one or the other
must get into us in the right measure.

That is also how it is with the earth, gentlemen. But however far you may have travelled, you will never yet have
seen, nor will the real globe-trotters, world travellers, have
been able to see anywhere that the earth cooked something
for itself, cooked its own midday meal! But it feeds itself
nevertheless, with substances exchanged all the time, for
the earth principle is all the time rising up in mists and
vapours. And you know that the rain water that comes

down is distilled, that it is pure water, with nothing in it. But the earth feeds itself in a subtle way out of cosmic space. It does not need to take meals. We human beings, having emancipated from the earth to some degree, need to obtain our foods from the earth. The earth itself feeds on the subtle forms of matter that are present everywhere in the universe. It is eating all the time, only we do not notice it, because it eats in such a subtle way. But you see, someone who looks at a human being in a fairly rough and ready way also does not notice that he is all the time taking in oxygen. In the same way we do not notice that the earth is all the time taking in food from cosmic space.

Well, gentlemen, we human beings take our meals. We eat foods through the stomach down into the lower body. That is perfectly, terribly obvious. But when it comes to our breathing it gets less obvious. And the social questions that come up also may be obvious. Everyone wants a good life; social questions arise in regard to what is obvious. But our social questions become less obvious when it comes to the air which we all breathe. There it cannot be done so easily that one takes it away from another; it can be done to some extent, but not so easily. In our lower body we are quite distinct from the earth. In our breathing we become more like the earth; it happens in a way that is less obvious. The fact is that we are continually not only hearing with our ears but also taking in iron; we absorb iron in a most subtle way. We take in light through the eyes but also substances all the time. You can see this in people who do not have these substances. We take in enormous amounts of matter especially through the nose, without noticing it. In our lower body we have emancipated from the earth, freed ourselves. There we can only take in foods produced by the earth, compacted and made more dense by it. We are able to take in air as it is in cosmic space. And in our head, in the senses, we keep wholly to the earth. We take in nutrients from the universe the way the earth itself does. The head is not for nothing a sphere, shaped like the earth. It deals with cosmic space the same way the earth does. But down below gravity comes in. There the human body develops towards the earth. Physical hands — gravity pulls downwards. Gravity does not have much influence on the head; it stays round. This is also why we must move on from the visible to the invisible there. We have to say to ourselves: flatfish would perish in spite of eating fish and crabs — for the fish and crabs are only of use to the pale, flat lower body — if they did not make themselves one-sided and, in a way, take in what comes from cosmic space. These are the beautiful, the subtle connections, gentlemen, that allow us to look into the laws and secrets of the universe, as it were.

Something the science of the spirit has to bring to mind again and again is that the real laws are perceived not with crude, but with subtle observation.

We'll continue at 9 o'clock on Wednesday. If you have questions, ask them.

Human clothing

Good morning, gentlemen. Have you perhaps thought of something you would like to have for today?

Mr Burle: *If one might ask Dr Steiner perhaps about human clothing, the garments people wear. In some countries people have just a rag that they wrap around them; others are buttoned up. One has shimmering colours, the other simple colours. Then one might also ask about the national costumes worn by a nation or by particular people. And also what waving flags are and – this may be connected with this – what ecstasy it causes?*

Rudolf Steiner: Concerning human clothing – people have often thought, as you can imagine, why it is that there are so few documents and historical records about it.

You see the clothes worn by simpler nations and tribes, and you also see the clothes worn by the people in the town where you yourself are at home. And finally one sees what one is putting on oneself, really paying least attention to the things one wears oneself. One simply goes along with custom in this. Indeed, to some extent one simply has to do this because otherwise one might be taken for half a fool if not a complete fool.

Now I think you'll agree the first question is the one that is probably hardest to answer for scientists considering only outer aspects, because, as I said, there are few written records about the reasons why people originally put on clothes. If you really consider everything that is available in this direction, you have to say to yourself: yes, much of what there is with regard to clothing has clearly come from people's need to have protection, the need to protect themselves from the influences of the environment. You must remember that animals have their own protection. Animals are very largely protected from external influences, which cannot get through their pelt, their skin, and so on and reach the more delicate, softer parts of the organism.

You may ask yourselves why people do not have such natural protection. I am not going to give too much consideration to this question, which is asking for the reason why, for with nature it is not really quite justifiable to ask the reason why. Nature simply puts the creatures there, and one simply has to study how they present themselves. The question why is never quite justifiable. But we'll understand one another if in spite of this I say: how come that man has to go about as he is, unclothed by nature?

Another question we must ask is whether the natural covering which animals have by nature does not clearly relate to the less advanced mental organization of the animals. And that is so. You see, gentlemen, it really is the case that sometimes the parts that are most important in a living creature, an animal and also in the human being, do not appear to be the most important to outer appearances. We can mention several organs in the human organism that are very small indeed. If they are not the way they are supposed to be the whole human organism breaks up. Here in the thyroid glands, for instance, tiny organs lie on either side — I have mentioned them in another context before[13] — they are barely the size of a pinhead. Now one might think them to be less important. But if it should ever happen that someone needed a thyroid operation, a goitre operation, and the surgeon were clumsy enough to remove these tiny pinhead-sized organs as well, the whole organism would get sick. The individual would grow imbecile and gradually die of debility. Tiny organs the size of a pinhead thus have the greatest imaginable importance for the whole of human life. They have it because these organs secrete a subtle matter that must enter into the blood. The blood will be useless unless these organs are present and their secretions flow into the blood. You can see, therefore, that even organs to which one pays little attention in the whole system have the greatest imaginable importance for the individual in whom they are found.

Take animals with hairy pelts, for instance. Now you can imagine that a pelt is useful to prevent the animals being cold in winter, and so on. And yes, it is useful for this. But for those hairs to develop in the skin the animal must be exposed to very strong sun influences. The hair develops in no other way but that the animal is exposed to powerful sun influences.

Now you might say: 'Yes, but the hairs develop not only in the places that are reached by the sun's rays.' But it is true, nevertheless. It even goes so far that the human embryo is hairy in the early stages when it is carried in the mother's womb. There you may say: 'It is not exposed to the sun.' The embryo later loses that hair. Why is that so? It is so because the mother takes in the sun's influence and this is active inside her. Hair is very closely connected with the sun's influence.

Take the lion, for example. Lions—and the males have that huge mane—are very much exposed to the sun. This also gives them chest organs that grow particularly strong under the sun's influence. The intestine is quite short, and the lungs are tremendously developed. The lion differs in this from our ruminants, in whom the organs of the lower body, intestines, stomach, and so on, are more developed. The way in which an animal has hair, feathers, and so on, thus relates above all to the sun's influence.

Yet again, if the sun's influence on a life form is very great then this life form allows the sun to think within it, to will in it—it does not become independent. Human beings are independent because they do not have this outer protection but are more or less exposed to their earthly environment. It is indeed interesting to note that animals are less dependent on the earth than humans are. Animals are largely created from outside the earth. I have provided evidence of this for you everywhere. But human beings are emancipated from these outside natural influences. And that is because they have an unprotected skin, as it were, in all directions, and must find their own protection.

Looking at the clothes we ordinarily wear you can see that there are two parts to them. One part is evident from the fact that in winter we put on a winter coat to protect us from the cold. This is the part of our clothing where we seek protection. But it is not the only part. You can see for instance, especially in women, that they look not only for protection in their clothes but also arrange them in a way they find beautiful. It may often be horrible, but it is supposed to be beautiful. This is a matter of taste or lack of taste, but it is meant to be beautiful, to adorn. These are the two functions of our clothing — to provide protection from the outside world and to adorn.

One of these functions has developed more in the north, where people need protection. There the clothing that is worn has more of a protect-yourself character. People actually do not go to great lengths when it comes to protection. But in warmer regions, regions where whole nations go about practically naked, really, the decorative aspect makes up the little, or if they put on more garments, the main part of their clothing.

You no doubt know that higher civilization has actually come from the warmer regions, that more of the life of mind and spirit has come from warmer regions. Considering the clothes people wear, we can therefore always see that in a sense the type of clothing designed to protect people from outside influences has remained imperfect. The clothing designed to adorn, on the other hand, has been developed in all kinds of ways. Now it is of course a question of people's taste, as you'll agree. The whole inner attitude of people comes into this. Let us think of more primitive peoples who are less sophisticated and more aboriginal. Such peoples have a great sense of colour. In our regions, where we are, of course, far advanced in intellect — or at least consider ourselves to be so — we do not have the sense of colour that the more aboriginal peoples have.

But those more aboriginal peoples also have a sense for something very different. They have a sense for it that human beings have supersensible, spiritual aspects. People in 'civilized' parts of the world no longer believe today that there are people who may not be as clever as civilized people consider themselves to be but have a sense for it that human beings have a supersensible aspect. And they sense this aspect in colour. That is how it is with those simple peoples, they sense that there is a supersensible aspect to them — I have called it the astral body — and sense its colours, and they want to make this invisible part of themselves visible. So they adorn themselves in red or blue, depending on whether they see themselves as blue or whatever in the astral sphere. This comes from the view of themselves that comes to these people from the world of the spirit.

The Greeks, for instance, saw that the human ether head is much bigger than the physical head, that it projects, and they therefore endowed the goddess Pallas Athene with a kind of helmet. But if you look at Pallas Athene and examine the helmet she is wearing you can see that the helmet has something like eyes at the top. You can see this everywhere; just look at Pallas Athene, even a poor quality statue, and you see eyes up there on the helmet. This proves to you that people believed it was really part of the body. It is something one is also able to see; they put it on Athene.

And the kind of clothing people created in regions where they had a feeling for the supersensible human being was made to show how they saw this human astral body.

Now in our regions—you know this, gentlemen—only ritual garments are arranged to be really colourful. If you look at the ritual garments, they are certainly arranged according to the way people saw the astral body with their inner eye. The colours used and the design of the garments basically derive from the supersensible sphere. And it is only if we understand this that we understand to what extent clothing is made decorative. This is also most important. If you look at pictures painted by the old masters you see that Mary, for instance, always wears a particular kind of dress and a particular kind of over-garment. This is meant to indicate the nature of her astral body, her heart and soul. This is meant to be indicated by her clothes. Compare pictures where Mary appears together with Mary Magdalene, you will always find that the old masters saw Mary and Mary Magdalene in a different light by the way they presented them, for this was thought to lie in their astral bodies, and the garments were painted to indicate the colour nature of the astral body.

We civilized people have entered more deeply into materialism, and no longer have a feeling for this supersensible aspect of the human being. We think with our earthly intellect and think the earthly intellect is master of it all. Indeed, gentlemen, this is also why we no longer have any feeling about dressing in a way that the clothes we wear would make us look at least half-way human! We put our legs—if we are men—into tubes. That is probably the plainest kind of garment you can have, this trouser tube! But we do much more; if we want to be particularly posh we stick a stove-pipe on our heads. Just imagine the face of an ancient Greek, if he were able to rise and someone would come towards him who has stuck his legs into two tubes and, what is more, has a tall stove-pipe up there, and what makes it even worse, in black! The Greek would not think this was a human being but an unbelievable spectre. This is something we must think about. And it even goes so far that one cuts away pieces of the coat, which is ugly enough as it is, and then calls it a tail coat. This is something which shows more than anything how thoughtless humanity has become. It is just because we are used to it, and, as I said, you are considered half a fool if not a complete fool if you do not join in, that we do join in with this. But we have to be aware that the whole way men dress today does rather remind one of a madhouse, especially when it is supposed to be utterly normal. It does show that people have gradually left all reality behind.

Women—and many men used to think they were less civilized than men—have adhered more to the original ways with their clothing. But there is a trend today to make women's clothing more like men's clothing, only it has not quite worked out so far.

To adorn—what does it mean, really? To present oneself outwardly in such a way that one also gives expression to what the human being is in spirit! To see how everything connected with clothing developed in more aboriginal nations we have to realize, in this respect, that among those aboriginal nations people did not feel themselves to be as independent as people today feel themselves to be independent. Today everyone feels himself an independent person, quite rightly so in some respects. Now you see, he will say to himself: 'I have my own mind and use it to think of everything I am able to do.' If he is particularly conceited, he will immediately see himself as a reformer, and so we have almost as many reformers today as there are people in the world. People thus consider themselves to be absolutely individual. No such thing existed among earlier peoples and tribes. Those tribes saw themselves to be at one as a group, with a spiritual entity their group soul. They considered themselves part of the group, like the members of a body, and the group soul was to them the element that kept them together. Within this group sphere they thought themselves to have quite a specific configuration, and they brought this to expression in the clothes they wore. So if they thought of their group soul as having a helmet-like extension to the head, as in Greece, for example, they would wear a helmet (Fig. 12). And that helmet did not develop from any need for protection, but because people believed they would be more like their group soul if they wore a helmet.

Fig. 12

In the same way some group souls were thought to be eagles, vultures or other animals, owls, and so on. People then organized their clothing accordingly, decorating it with feathers or the like, so that they would be similar to the group soul. Clothes thus evolved largely to meet the spiritual needs of people.

Among the aboriginal nations and tribes the clothes showed a little bit how they imagined their group soul to be. And when you find an aboriginal nation and ask yourself how they dress, and above all adorn themselves, do they adorn themselves with feathers or an animal skin, you can say that if you find a tribe that adorns itself mainly with feathers, you know their common group soul, their guardian spirit, as it were, was thought to be a bird. If you find that a nation adorns itself mainly with animal skins, they imagined their group soul, their guardian spirit, as it were, to be a lion or a tiger or something of this kind. We can therefore find out something about the original clothes people wore by asking ourselves how those people envisaged their group soul.

And Mr Burle was quite right when he said that some wear floating garments, others close-fitting ones. Floating garments evolved because people wanted to make bird-clothes, garments with wings; it pleased them to have something winglike. And it actually had a great effect on people's skill development to acquire such floating garments. And when they rotated they would also make pleasing movements with their arms. This made them skilful and so on. So we may well say: to adorn oneself is to have the will to bring something spiritual to expression in the clothes worn at the time. And merely to protect oneself — and this is not, of course, to say anything against it — gives expression to the uninspired aspect of the human being. The more one seeks to use clothes that serve only to protect, the more one is lacking in inspiration. The more one seeks to adorn oneself, the less does one lack in inspiration, really wanting to give expression to the spiritual quality to be found in the dignity of man.

It is perfectly natural that these things shifted completely in later stages of civilization. We have to be clear about the following, for instance. Imagine those early peoples discovering that the sun has a special influence on the human heart, the human chest altogether, and saying to themselves: 'I am a person with heart only because the sun is able to have the right influence. Not outwardly, on the skin, for then I would be completely hairy, but when they are inwardly digested, the sun's rays act on the heart.' The heart is quite rightly seen in relation to the actions of the sun. What did people do who still were very much alive to knowledge of this connection with the sun? Well, you see, they tied a kind of medallion around their necks, a medallion representing the sun (Fig. 13). They would wear this to say: 'I make it known that the sun has an influence on the heart.'

Fig. 13

Later on this would be forgotten, of course. Civilized people have forgotten that this was originally a sign that the sun has an influence on the heart. But something which once had meaning has become habit, truly a habit. And people then put on such things from habit, no longer having any idea why it was worn originally. Such habits develop first of all; later governments lay claim to them, making them their possession. This is essentially all there is to the so-called 'advancement' of states and governments — they take possession of things that have become habit. Someone discovers — only a human being can discover it — a medicine, let us say. This arises from his mind and spirit. The government then lays claim to this medicine for itself, saying: 'It may only be sold in one place or another with my permission.' In the end, therefore, it comes from the government.

That is also what happened to the sun medallion. People originally created and wore it from personal knowledge, and later out of habit. Then the governments said: 'Oh no, you cannot do this of your own accord, but we must first give you permission to create and wear it.' And that is how medals and decorations developed. Today governments adorn their adherents with medals. Medals have of course lost all meaning by now. But anyone who grumbles about medals and decorations should also know that they did have real meaning originally, that they have evolved from something that had meaning.

You see, that is what has happened with many of the original garments. The ancient Romans and Greeks still knew that if they went about showing their naked bodies that would not be the whole human being, for there was also a supersensible body. They imitated this supersensible body in the toga, and that is how the toga was created. The Romans therefore wanted to reproduce the supersensible body. The toga is nothing but the astral body. And the folds so skilfully made in the garment showed the forces of the astral body. People of modern times, no longer having any knowledge of the real spiritual human being, knew no better than to take the old garments and, in order to have something new, cut off little bits here and there, first shortening the part that came close to the ground, and then making it as far as possible a garment you could slip into, and gradually changing it until it had become the modern man's jacket. The modern man's jacket is nothing but the chopped-up toga of old, only one does not recognize it as such.

Take belts, for instance. Now, the belt developed because people knew they were divided off in the middle in a way no animal is divided. No animal has the kind of diaphragm that human beings have, for example. And this division in the middle does not have the significance in any animal which it has in human beings. Just look at it and compare. People are forgetting about this today in the most incredible way. So they often compare the length of a person with that of an animal in order to establish something or other, for instance how much food an animal and a human being needs. But just think: there you have an animal, and there a human being (Fig. 14). Someone measures the length of the animal and the length of a human being. Well, gentlemen, can we compare the two? That is nonsense. The length measured in the animal is only *this* part in the human being. You can therefore only compare the length a person has from the top of the head down to the lumbar part, here, to compare it with the animal world. Or if you want to compare *this* part of the human being with the animal you can compare it with the two hind limbs of the animal. It is really true that thoughtlessness often goes a very long way.

Now when primitive people became aware of the significance of this division which humans have in the middle, they indicated this with a body belt. So here, too, a human property was indicated, by the body belt.

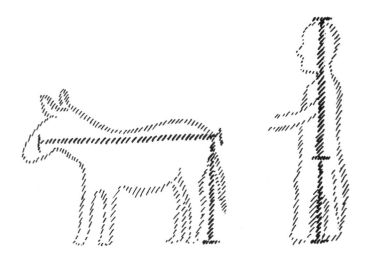

Fig. 14

And you see if the nature of the human being is truly recognized, one will know, for instance, that a special power actually relating to thinking lies in the crook of the knee. And the crook of the knee was therefore adorned — we can no longer decorate it specially today because it is covered by the trouser tube. This later became the Order of the Garter in the way I have described. All these things have evolved from genuine perceptions; they did not evolve in the terrible kind of abstract, theoretical thinking we have today.

And you see, modern clothes have also lost all their colour. The question is, why did they lose their colour? Because one's feeling for the supersensible is best expressed in colour. And the more people delight in colour, the more are they really inclined to grasp the supersensible in some way or other. Our age likes grey in grey, however, colours that are as colourless as possible. The reason for this may be indicated by the saying: 'When candles are away all cats are grey.' For modern people no longer look into the light at all, I mean the light of the spirit. Everything has become grey for them. And they show this most in their clothes. They no longer know what colour they should use to adorn themselves, and so they do not adorn themselves with any colour. One can really see that everything by way of clothing is connected with things people still knew in the past, when they knew about the supersensible human being. And civilization in general has turned grey. But for some purposes in life the original colourful nature has remained, though people do not know where it comes from.

The kind of clothes our military people wear in a modern nation have of course developed at a time when people increasingly needed to defend themselves. And you can examine every part of military clothing to see if it has some connection with means of defence or attack. Basically we may say that all military clothes are really obsolete today, for one no longer understands them. You see, the jacket of a modern suit can be understood, for it has developed out of the Roman toga. But a military uniform coat can only be understood if one explains it not in terms of a Roman toga, with its folds, that has been distorted into caricature, but out of medieval knighthood, when the whole was a kind of cuirass. The cuirass has been reshaped.

Flags were also mentioned (as part of the question). You see, the situation concerning flags is this. Originally the heraldic animal would be depicted on the flag — it need not necessarily have been an animal. But what was this animal? It was the group soul, the soul that kept people together. And they wanted to have an image of it before them when they were together as a group. They made it into a flag. And flags actually are proof that common ideas people had were used to create their flag.

Here it is particularly important to be clear in our minds that the old masters were much closer to reality in their work than modern painters. Today people paint pictures which are framed and hung somewhere because that is what one has got used to. Basically it is meaningless. Why should one hang a picture on a wall? That is the question we must ask. In earlier times it was like this. People had altars, and they painted the image on the altar that should come to mind when one stood before the altar. They had churches, and people walked about in them. On the walls they painted the things that should come to mind one after the other as one walked around. This had meaning. It related to what went on in people's minds.

And in the knights' castles of old — well, what was the knighthood based on in those days? It was based on the fact that its members always looked up to their ancestors. The ancestors were more important to them than they were themselves. Someone who had a great many ancestors counted more. And so they would hang up paintings of their ancestors. And again it had meaning.

It was only when this meaning was lost that landscape painting evolved. And landscape painting—to have a landscape hanging on your wall, well, you know, it is something people may like. I do not want to be at all horrible in this respect and decry all landscape painting, but you have to accept that a painted landscape can never be the same as when you go out into the landscape yourself! And landscape painting really only began to develop when people no longer had any real feeling for nature.

If you look at paintings done just a few centuries ago—yes, take a look also at paintings by Raphael or Leonardo[14]—and you'll see that they painted people. The landscape is just hinted at, quite childlike really, because people agreed that landscapes should be looked at outside, in nature. One can, however, bring a great deal to expression in a human being; man is not just nature, and one can bring different things to expression. And so Raphael was able to bring much to expression in Mary. You may know the painting that is in Dresden—Mary with the Jesus child on her left arm, with clouds above. And then there are two figures down below—Pope Sixtus IV and St Barbara. This is the painting known as the *Sistine Madonna*. Well, gentlemen, Raphael did not paint this picture so that it might be hung somewhere but he actually only painted Mary with the Jesus child so that a banner might be made to be carried ahead of processions. They had these processions where people go out into the fields to an altar, and they always had a banner that was carried before them. They would stop at the altar, where people would kneel down. Later on someone added the saints Sixtus and Barbara. They do not at all belong in the picture, and the quality of the painting is terrible compared to Raphael's own work. But people don't notice this. Some admire the somewhat repulsive figure of Barbara in this painting just as much as they admire what Mary and the Jesus child themselves are!

All these things show you that people have moved away from the things that gave meaning to painting. Why did Raphael paint this picture for a church banner? Because people were to have this common idea as they went in the procession—which was in accord with the feeling out of which flags and banners were actually produced.

Then the desire arose to give at least some kind of meaning to things that have come down to us from earlier times, when they did have real meaning. Going to some places today, to Finland, for instance, you will see people wearing the old clothes again. People who especially want to be members of their nation wear the old garments again that had been forgotten and are now brought back again.

But people no longer live in the times when the old instincts were there that gave those clothes their meaning. Today we would have to find a way of dressing that arises from the life of mind and spirit we have today, just as those earlier peoples found their way of dressing out of what lived in their minds, out of what they felt to be the right way of dressing, considering the world and the human race. But people are no longer able to do this today because they know nothing of the real—that is, the spiritual—human being. And so it has happened that we wear garments today that really are quite meaningless and simply come into existence merely because meaninglessness is taken to extremes.

People originally wore belts to show that this was a special area. The belt was used to express this. Later on, people saw the belt, say that the person was divided at that point; they then made this division themselves using a belt. Instead of expressing something, the belt often made women's garments such that they did not express some-thing but tremendously compressed the liver and the stomach and all kinds of things here. It is fair to say that much of what has developed in the materialist age has developed from lack of meaning, in utter meaninglessness. Things we have to recognize as nonsense today did have a particular meaning among primitive peoples. Let us assume, for instance, that some wild tribes have the peculiarity that they do not clothe themselves by pulling on garments but in some other way. A garment is really something, you'll agree, that adorns, adding something to what the human being is. The significance of the garment is really suggestion, revelation. The invisible is thus to be revealed in the garment. And the wild tribes thought—they still do so today, and so do other people—one does not necessarily need fabrics to clothe oneself, one can also dress by making all kinds of drawings on the body. They adorn themselves by tattooing, as it is called. People thus make all kinds of marks on their bodies.

Well, gentlemen, those signs which people drew on their bodies originally had great significance. Let us assume, for example, someone scratches a heart shape on his body. This has no significance when he is awake, walking about during the day. But when he is sleeping, this heart scratched into the skin makes a highly significant impression on the sleeping soul, and becomes a thought in the sleeping soul, a thought he will of course have forgotten when he returns to conscious awareness in the morning. Tattooing therefore originally developed out of the intention to influence the human being even in sleep. This, too, lost significance later, even among primitive peoples, at least to the extent that people do it only from habit, continuing out of habit, but it has lost its meaning.

Now you see, you have to take all these things into account. You will then see that clothes developed partly from a desire for protection, and in the main part, most of all, from a desire to adorn oneself. And this adornment has to do with people making the supersensible outwardly apparent. And it then happened specifically with regard to clothing that people gradually knew no more than that one wears them. And that is how national costumes developed. Obviously people for whom there was greater necessity to protect themselves would have close-fitting garments, thick garments, weighing the whole body down, more or less, with garments, or at least the parts that were more exposed to the cold. Someone living in a warmer climate would develop the decorative aspect much more strongly, would be wearing thinner garments, floating garments, and so on. It would to some extent depend on the whole environment, on the climate, how people partly protected and partly adorned themselves. Then people forgot about this. When tribes began to migrate it could happen that a people coming from a region where the clothing was appropriate to the region moved to another region where one really could not see why this kind of clothing should be suitable for these people—but they kept them from habit. And so it is often very difficult today to discover why people wear a particular kind of clothing by just considering their immediate environment. And we can see, can't we, that people are simply no longer thinking. They are like a polar bear who is given a white garb because this does not stand out much from the snows in the Arctic and therefore means protection from pursuit and so on. Well, if the polar bear were to wear this in a warm climate it clearly would not offer protection!

That is the way it is altogether. People stick to the things they are used to without being fully aware of their meaning. Because of this it is not so easy today to know from the way people dress why a particular nation dresses in a particular way. As I said, we have to go back to earlier times for this.

You'll find, for instance, that the Magyar costume worn in Hungary is something quite special. The Hungarians wear fairly high boots with narrow shafts, close-fitting trousers inserted in those shafts, and a jacket that fits closely.

Everything has been modernized, has lost its original meaning, but it indicates something that is also evident in the Hungarian language, for its original terms are largely hunting terms. It is really strange. If you go to Pest, for example, you may, as you cross the road, see a sign that says: *Kave Ház*. This is nothing other than 'Coffee House'! It is not Hungarian or Magyar, of course, but comes from the German *Kaffeehaus*, with just minor changes. People will say *Kave Ház* without realizing that it is really a German word. But if one leaves aside the many words coming from the Latin or German in Magyar, one realizes the language consists largely of hunting terms, and that the Magyars were originally hunters. And if you consider the costume, you see that it is a style that was originally the most comfortable for hunters. It then came to be modernized and changed. There you can still understand it, at a pinch. But when one sees the clothes people wear today, one cannot understand anything very much.

Now, Mr Burle, have some things become clear with the things I have said?

Mr Burle: Fairly!

Now, we'll continue with the lectures next Saturday. Perhaps the one or the other of you will still think of something you'd like to ask.

Effects of arsenic and alcohol

Good morning, gentlemen. Is there anything special you would like to have today?

Mr Müller: Yes, a small query. Dr Steiner recently spoke about arsenic and very large children. Years ago I always saw such large children at the fair. I realized afterwards that the children who were shown at the fair had been at most 8, 12 or 16 years old. Children artificially brought to that state would sometimes come from Hungary. And since Dr Steiner said that arsenic is commonly found in the rocks there, I would like to ask what age such children may reach, children who have been artificially brought up on arsenic to make them large. Would it not be possible to take people who bring up children on arsenic to court and get the law to forbid people to do such things? Or is it only done very secretly as a source of business?

Dr Steiner mentioned that people who were able to stop the arsenic at a certain stage did come down again. That was not the case with these children; these were children who weighed about two hundredweight although they were only about 16. Surely they would have a difficult future ahead?

Dr Steiner also spoke about alcohol, that we produce alcohol in our bodies, and about the different effects of alcohol. One person gets extremely upset, making a row, and so on, and another is very quiet. Yet another has problems with his eyes, which is what happens to me. After one, two, three glasses I have hard granules in my eyes the next morning that one can hardly squash with one's fingers, as the result of taking alcohol.

Then Dr Steiner also said that one could, as it were, detect all diseases in the eyes. Now there are also people who say they can recognize all diseases by just looking at the urine. There is someone like that in Basel; would that be right? I can't believe it.

I'd also like to ask how it is when people get some medicine somewhere and firmly believe in it – would that contribute to the cure?

Then I'd also refer to Dr Steiner's last but one talk, about fresh water. There's a pond near Darmstadt where hot water comes in all the time from the chemical industry – it is actually steaming – and in this pond are thousands and thousands of goldfish and every one of them is dark red all over. How does that happen? They are dark red all over.

Rudolf Steiner: So the first question was about the fatty children.

It is true, as you thought quite rightly, that these children who are shown in all kinds of fair booths as something remarkable are fattened up artificially with arsenic or similar substances—you see, many other substances are similar to arsenic. And they are not particularly strong, those children, as one could test quite easily, but are merely fat, large.

Now you see, there is something much more complicated involved than what I said recently about adults taking arsenic. What I said then had to do with adults. They get into the kind of states I was speaking of. In these children, and it is indeed true that a crime is being committed against them—one cannot deny this—the action of the arsenic or similar substances is also due to something else. These children have to be treated in this criminal fashion at about the age I have always told you is an important period in life—in the years between the changing of the teeth, which would be their 6th or 7th year, and sexual maturity, which would be in their 14th or 15th year. And you see, at this age a child is not only such that one sends it to school, to the ordinary primary school, but something else happens as well.

You will remember, gentlemen, that I told you human beings consist not only of this physical body, which we see with our eyes and can touch with our hands, but also of supersensible soul and spirit aspects. One of the subtle bodies I called the human ether body. We have to consider this ether body in human development just as we do the physical body. To draw this rather schematically, we have the human being in his physical body (Fig. 15). But around this physical body and also inside it is this subtle body, the ether body. And apart from the physical body and the ether body — where even the ether body cannot be seen with our ordinary eyes — there is also the astral body in the human being, which is able to sense things. Plants still have an ether body, they can grow; that is because of the ether body. The human being and animals have an astral body; they can sense things, feel. Plants cannot do this. I told you that some people think a plant is able to feel; it definitely cannot.

Fig. 15

You see, gentlemen, with every substance that has an effect on human beings we must ask ourselves: on which of these different aspects does the substance have an effect? Arsenic acts particularly on the astral body and very powerfully on our breathing. Our breathing depends on the astral body. When one gives arsenic to someone, all the consequences which the arsenic has come by the roundabout route via the astral body.

When a person lives through the early years, from birth until, let us say, the changing of the teeth in the 7th or 8th year, it is mainly the physical human body which develops. You can see this physical body developing. Look at a very small baby that has only just been born. You'll not really be able to say at that time if he looks more like his father or his mother. You know how it is, with aunts and uncles coming to the house when such a child has been born. One will say: 'Oh, he's the spitting image of his mother—especially the feet!' Another comes and says: 'Looks exactly like his father.' That is the way it is. An infant has not developed in a decided way in his physical body, and it will only be later that one can see whom he resembles. Just look at the nose, a most expressive organ. The nose of a young infant may look very different from what it will be later on. This will be at a later time for some, but as a rule it is the case that when the changing of the teeth comes, the nose, which is relatively late in developing its proper form, its proper configuration, will have the right form.

Later, after the 7th or 8th year, the physical body really only increases in size, with the muscles getting stronger, but it has his actual form, its configuration, by the 7th year. The situation is, then, that it is mainly the physical body which comes to expression between the 1st and 7th years of life. And between the changing of the teeth and sexual maturity, between the 7th or 8th year and the 14th or 15th year, it is mainly the ether body which develops. This is the body that holds the powers of nutrition and growth. And the astral body only comes to develop between the 14th or 15th and the 20th or 21st years. It is only then that the astral body really develops. It is not that it would not be there before — we have it from birth — but the real development of the astral body happens only after the 14th or 15th year.

When an adult who has passed his 14th or 15th year is given arsenic, he has developed his astral body. The arsenic is taking effect in him, but the organism is able to resist a little. But when a child between the 7th and 15th year is given arsenic, the astral body has not been developed, and the full power of the arsenic is brought to bear on the child. No power of resistance exists in the organism at that time. And the result is that the arsenic action, which above all causes masses of fat to be deposited, with everything turning to fat, causes everything to become spherical, growing sideways between the 7th and the 14th or 15th year.

You have to consider that the things I am telling you have tremendous importance where life is concerned. I know every one of you may say: 'Oh well, you are telling us that arsenic given to a child between the 7th and 14th or 15th years plays a great role, making the child fat, spherical, but I know people who have grown extremely large from childhood without having been given extra arsenic.' Yes, gentlemen, but you have to consider that the substances that occur in nature may be found everywhere, at least in small amounts. And we may say that people cannot take nourishment, or a child cannot take nourishment, without taking something that contains arsenic. Arsenic is also present in our foods.

Now you know that children have different tastes, different preferences. One child likes to eat one thing, another something else. And there are children who have a real preference for foods that contain arsenic. Later in life it may also still happen that one gets fat from things one enjoys eating. If you eat things you do not like you get thin as a rake. If you eat things you enjoy and also have the time to give yourself up to it, you will get large and fat. This is especially so with children, and above all with children between the 7th and 14th or 15th years. If children have such a yen for foods that contain arsenic they get large and fat. But the children exhibited in fair booths and so on – as mentioned by Mr Müller – are given arsenic artificially, just as in Alpine regions, and this is also the case in Hungary, where arsenic is found in the rocks in the mountain areas. These children are therefore given arsenic, and the main thing is that the child develops a taste for arsenic exactly at this age. It is horrible, but it is so. The child gradually begins to desire this arsenic, as if it were sugar, and takes it, and it then happens that the child gets large and fat before its astral body has properly developed. And such children can be put on show because they are something abnormal, gaining a terrible amount of weight. And people then consider it something worth looking at. People always want to see things that are unusual, and what will people not do to offer others something they enjoy. There are also quite different things designed to give people pleasure.

There is something else, for example, which is done with boys at that same age. You know that the human voice changes at the time when sexual maturity is reached, in the 14th or 15th year. It changes in boys – in girls changes have more to do with breast development and so on. But with boys the voice changes. A bad practice – it had become a great art especially in ancient Rome – is to castrate boys to keep their voices boyish, really high voices. Castration means to cut out their sexual organs. This gives you the famous choir boys with their tremendously high voices. Now you see, that is an even worse practice. But it is done under the pretence of being for sacred purposes. I don't

know if you know it or not. So these things also exist, and
we have to understand that there have been such things in
this world, and that people really do all kinds of things so
that even human nature may become something for exhi-
bition and show.

If one considers the consequences of such things, it is like
this. When someone has been given this arsenic in his
young days and has grown large and fat, when the time
comes to develop his astral body it will be much too small
for the large body. It will be much too small and feeble. And
the result is that when sexual maturity is reached and the
astral body should begin to develop, this astral body is
indeed much too small and feeble for the large, fat body.
And children who have been fed arsenic in this way and
dragged around the show booths will then have an astral
body that is too small. And the result of this will be that
certain organs do not develop at all. The organs will be
flaccid then, completely flaccid. And it is above all the lungs
which grow flaccid in these children. This is sometimes
most painful to see, for in their 20th year or even earlier
these children get into a state where they really are no
longer able to breathe. This is not only because the lungs
drown in the fat but because they grow flaccid, having no
energy. And then comes a situation where something
special happens with the lung. You see, gentlemen, the lung
is not just an organ for breathing, the lung is also an
important organ of nutrition, and the lung has to be properly nourished if a person is to go on living in the right way.
Most lung diseases are not at all due to the breathing being
unhealthy but to the lung not being properly nourished.

In these children it is no longer properly nourished from
the 17th or18th year onwards, because fatty degeneration of
all the organs means that nutrients do not reach the lung at
all. They may be said to reach the lung last, although it
needs to be nourished. Foods go through all kinds of

changes in the human body, as I have shown you. They go through six or seven changes. And the lung needs foods that have been changed seven times, these most precious things. This transformation does not happen, however, in those children. Most of them are therefore dead by their early twenties. And it is absolutely true to say that children who are exhibited at fairs in this way will be dead by their early twenties. They either die of debility or they develop lung disease. Most of them die of lung disease. It is because of this that one does not see such people at a later stage, as you said, for they die before that.

It is of course difficult to take legal measures against such things. People should see to it that it stops, just as people should do more themselves to create the right kind of social life and not always scream for the law right away. But I am also convinced that very few people know about the things I have just told you, for example. Very few people know how much more harmful arsenic is at the very age when it is given to these children than later on in life, for example. And I still believe that if people are informed about these things then the matter will improve even without legislation, without coercion, without always cracking the whip. But how can things get better if one is unable to make the truth known!

I know you'll say: 'Well, we did not have much education, we cannot know this, but we are sure the university professors will know it.' They do not know it at all. They simply do not know. And this is why such things are not made known. And it is important that it is understood by as many people as possible. Such things should and must be known.

Something similar, though also very different, is the case with alcohol. We have talked about alcohol before. But of course in the case of this arsenic poisoning, which leads to fatty degeneration, someone else gives it to the children, and when an adult takes arsenic he really does so in full awareness. And it has to be said that here it would have a tremendous effect if people were informed. We might well say that someone who takes arsenic simply from vanity, as I have told you, could be given the information. And if he really understands the consequences he may well not do it. With alcohol, on the other hand, the problem is so great because enlightenment does not help much in this case — unless people stop taking alcohol altogether. For once they start and take one or two glasses they get into a state where enlightenment fades away, and they will then go on drinking. This is why it is particularly difficult to achieve much by informing people about alcohol. Enlightenment should of course be effective in this case, and the fact that this is exactly the area where one has to resort so much to the law is really a sad thing in terms of people's strength of mind. There are countries today — just think of North America — where laws actually forbid the import of alcohol, in order to make people be sensible. Well, if we get to the point where people will only be sensible, and altogether useful, if everything is prescribed by law, then the human race is not worth much any more here on earth.

The situation with alcohol is this. I have told you that human beings produce their own alcohol in their bodies. This is because they need alcohol to preserve themselves. And you can be sure, gentlemen, the alcohol you produce yourselves will never make you drunk! The amount is just as much as you need to preserve the foods in you, making things last that should last in you. You'll realize the purpose, of course, of the alcohol we produce ourselves. You'll also have seen here or there that to preserve a dead animal, or some part of the human body, it is no good to leave it exposed to the air, and it has to be put in spirits, into alcohol. Alcohol thus keeps the form and structure of living things that have died. This is altogether a most important law of nature. What happens when you leave living things that have died to nature? The human body begins to perish the moment it is given over to the earth, it is dissolved. And that is how it is with all living things. The moment the ether body has left a living thing, that thing is destroyed, except if one uses such means as alcohol. Alcohol thus has the power to keep together those other powers that keep living things together.

You can see from this that alcohol is not earthly. There is also something else that will show you that alcohol is not earthly in the ordinary way. The human body and the animal body and the plant body are destroyed by the earthly element, but they are preserved, as we say, kept from being destroyed, by alcohol.

But how does alcohol come into existence? Well, you just have to look at a grape vine. Alcohol develops in the very place where the sun is able to shine most on the vine. And you know that grape vines do not thrive in northern Germany, for it gets too cold there, and the sun no longer has the power that is needed. If you draw a line parallel to the equator through Gruenberg in Silesia — very few people get drunk on Gruenberger wine, for it's as sour as may be! Wine can only be produced in places where the sun has that power on plants. Wine is therefore produced not by something earthly, but exactly by something from beyond the earth, the sun principle, something that is beyond the earth. People need to be altogether very cautious about taking in things that come from beyond this earth.

How does it happen that people produce their own alcohol inside? It happens like this, and I am going to tell you something that will probably interest you especially, only one has to pay a bit of attention to understand it. You see, where is solar energy, gentlemen? Solar energy exists in everything the sun shines on. Do observe — let's make it really easy to see. On a really hot summer day I put my chair out there in the burning sun, and leave it there for some hours before inviting you to take a seat. You sit down on the chair. Wow, you think, that's got really hot! Now I think you'll agree it is not a case of the sun shining on the particular organ, making you feel hot. If you had stood in the same place for that length of time, assuming the appropriate posture, the organ in question would have got as hot as the chair, and you would have felt it in your own body. But that is not the case; the chair has got hot. So you see, an ordinary, lifeless body has taken up the sun's heat and then passed it on to you.

It is much more complicated in the case of coal. Anthracite has been a palm tree or some other tree thousands and thousands of years ago. How did it come about? Well, there you had the earth (Fig. 16) and there a palm tree or a palmlike tree, with the sun shining on it. It later perished and went down into the soil. But just as the sun's heat was stored in the chair, so did the sun's heat stay in the palm

Fig. 16

tree, going into the soil with it. The palm tree turns into coal; the sun's heat stays in it. And thousands of years later you dig up the coal, put it in your stove, and the sun's heat is given back to you. You are heating your rooms today with heat from the sun when it shone on the earth thousands of years ago. People often do not think of this. When you sit on a chair and it warms your bottom you still notice that the sun left something of its energy there. With anthracite you no longer notice it. So you have to say: where anthracite is found in the earth, everywhere where there is anthracite, we have very ancient solar energy. The coal or carbon deposits everywhere are full of very ancient solar energy.

Well, gentlemen, you do however eat plants. You put them inside you. Your own organism acts faster than the earth; the life-filled carbon from the plants is quickly converted and you then have carbon dioxide in your own body, which contains a lot of carbon. This carbon dioxide you have inside you does not turn to coal like the anthracite underground, but remains carbon dioxide. In the carbon dioxide you now have carbon, which you have inside you, and oxygen which comes from the air and also from foods. It is called carbon and oxygen. And you also have hydrogen in the human body, for you drink water, for example. This hydrogen combines with the carbon and the oxygen. And you only have to think of something you also have in a human body, something that begins to get smelly under certain conditions. And you only have to think of something that comes from animal bodies, which is eggs—we spoke of this the other day[15]—they get smelly. That is nitrogen. Only it does not smell when it is in the air, for there it is combined with other substances in a particular way.

Now you see, gentlemen, you walk about, need oxygen, carbon, nitrogen in order to live, and produce alcohol inside your organism. Alcohol is produced in the human organism to prevent us falling apart inside. The body would dissolve, just as it dissolves when it is a corpse, unless alcohol and alcohol-like compounds are produced. That is a natural thing. But now we must ask: on which of our bodies does alcohol act? You see, taken in moderate amounts alcohol initially has a very good effect on the physical body, for someone who produces too little alcohol can gain a good preservative with alcohol, and the alcohol does not really harm the physical body. Basically alcohol does not have at all a bad effect on the physical body. If alcohol were to harm the physical body – people do not give enough thought to this – the vine would be in a poor way, for the vine also has a physical body. The vine is completely blotto – it is this because it is full of alcohol – but its physical body does not suffer. Well, and the ether body also does not suffer from alcohol. Only the astral bodies of adult people are harmed by alcohol. It is equally harmful in children, as I'll tell you in a minute, because something else happens as well. But in adults alcohol also affects the astral body, just like arsenic, and above all the I. And the I lives in the blood circulation. Alcohol therefore has a powerful effect on the blood circulation.

Alcohol is so bad for children because it already has an astral body inside it. Plants only have an ether body, but the alcohol that is in the vine does have an astral body. This acts just like the principle that bubbles and boils in the blood. Is this hard to understand? Surely you can understand this. It acts like the principle that bubbles and boils in the blood. And this is also why children who drink alcohol at an early age get an astral body that they should really only develop fully by their 14th or 15th year; and they have no control over it. This is why alcohol is particularly harmful for children, because children will immediately get an astral body under the influence of alcohol.

You can see from this that alcohol really influences the

soul sphere, the mind of the human being. That is where it is active. It destroys the breathing, the blood circulation, which arise from the sphere of mind and soul. These are affected by alcohol.

Now you should not think that the human head is a separate organ in the human being, and the chest, too, a separate organ. For although human beings are threefold, everything also influences everything else. Not only the lower body has to be nourished but especially also the human head. And when someone drinks alcohol and has the kind of lower body where alcohol is especially well processed—let us say someone is well able to tolerate two, three glasses of alcohol. I am not sure if that is what Mr Müller wanted to say of himself? But you probably tolerate a small amount of alcohol quite well?

Mr Müller denied this, saying that the granules appeared the next morning even if he had just one glass of beer.

So it is really the opposite in your case; you really do not tolerate alcohol at all?

Mr Müller confirmed that this was so.

Well, in that case you are an example of those who do not tolerate alcohol well. Now you see, if someone does not tolerate alcohol that well, does not really digest the alcohol that well, then the undigested alcohol reaches the head, also influencing the eyes, and causing mucous matter to push up towards the head. The blood is set boiling in someone who tolerates alcohol well, and in someone who does not tolerate it well the mucous material starts to move, and the mucus condenses towards the outside, so that it becomes granular. It is mucous material that has condensed. This is what can happen to someone who really does not tolerate even the first glass of alcohol that well. But let us assume someone is able to take a lot. Then the thing also goes to the head, but into the blood; and then you do not get those granules, and the whole blood circulation in the head is stimulated, and the whole blood circulation of the head secretes substances which are harmful. You then get the general inebriation, the general hangover, and a person gets to a state where he goes on and on drinking. So this is how one can tell the effect of alcohol on one person and on another.

You see, one would like to say: we really should have no need to tell these things apart, to look for them so hard, for whatever the situation may be, if alcohol has particularly abnormal effects it is really best to leave it alone. It is not good to go on taking alcohol when one feels the effects of it.

But, as I said, alcohol acts on the astral body and the I today. The I feels stimulated. A person likes the taste of alcohol and he really feels that there is something in alcohol that takes him beyond earthly concerns. This feeling is really very interesting, for as I had to tell you, alcohol does not come from the earth but from a sphere that is not earthly. This is also why a person feels lifted above the earthly realm. Alcohol becomes a cure for cares, does it not? With alcohol a person is taken a bit beyond himself, and it feels infinitely good to be a bit outside oneself. And it is this which leads to widespread alcohol abuse.

Now there was another question for us to consider. Mr Müller said, if I understood you rightly, that there is a pond near Darmstadt and that warm industrial effluents pass through this pond? You can see what this is about from what I have been saying before. On the last but one occasion I tried to show you that when I say the fish in the sea do not have direct sun, this does not mean you should think they get no sun influence at all. Just as coal in the ground still holds the sun's effects thousands and thousands of years later, so does water also still have the sun's effects in it. And there, we have to say, the fish merely have to be organized in a different way compared to animals that live on land. And you can of course see that fish are organized differently. If fish had the kind of lungs that other animals and humans have, they could not live in water, of course. As you know, higher animals and human beings will simply drown if they live permanently in water. So they cannot live there. Fish can live there because they do not have lungs but gills; with these they get the air into themselves that is in the water and always has solar energies in it.

Now you know how people keep goldfish. You can't keep them in ordinary water; there you simply won't have goldfish. If there is shade you can at most breed them, but not keep them. The offspring take their colour from the old goldfish if you want to keep them without sun. But you'll find, if you keep goldfish in water that has no sun, that they get very pale after three or four months. The little goldfish get their proper bright colour if there is direct sun in their water. That is a difference. You see, if I have a pond here, or even a small basin, and the sun shines directly into it (Fig. 17), something else is there for the fish than in another place. Here it has to use old solar energies that have been in the water for some time; here it gains new solar energies that have been in the water for a shorter time.

Now the Darmstadt factory that lets its warm water run into the pond is a special case. You have to admit that when something has been under some restraint where life is concerned and then is free again, it will really wriggle a

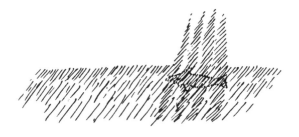

Fig. 17

great deal and develop. Imagine how it would be if you had tied a person down for some time. He cannot move a limb when he is locked up. When he is free again he takes a special pleasure and enjoyment in life. And now think of the water from the Darmstadt factory running into the pond. This water is getting its solar influence in a very special way. The factory basically also runs on coal, for everything goes back to coal. The heat used in it comes from coal. Coal has preserved solar energies through thousands and thousands of years. These solar energies now enter the pond as warm water. And it is indeed the case that solar energies which are released after having been locked up in the coal for thousands of years are particularly active. So you can't do better than to let those active solar energies run into the pond with the warm water. One might even do this artificially. One might artificially arrange things in such a way that one pours warm water into the ponds where goldfish are kept. And especially if you let the water move, so that the solar energies are set in motion, they will stimulate the goldfish to develop a really lively colour.

You could make the following experiment. Imagine you have a large artificial pool. You first let warm water run into it, to remain motionless at the bottom, and then add ordinary water on top. And then you put in the goldfish. Now take another artificial pool and run in warm water so that there is a continuous stream of it going in. Now see which fish have the more lively golden yellow colour — not those in calm water but those that have warm water flowing through all the time, for that keeps the energies alive.

In the case of that industrial concern this happens of its own accord, with new warm water running in all the time. So it is not at all surprising that the goldfish do especially well. That is the way nature works. One has to understand these things properly and then one discovers these ways in which nature works.

Now you will say to yourselves: what is it that is so active in the rays of the sun? Well, gentlemen, that is the ether which is also active in our own ether bodies. The ether is active in the sun's rays. And just as the ether is needed to stimulate the astral in us, so it is also out there in the natural world.

The vine has its ether body inside it. Because it is touched by the sun's heat, something astral is created in it, really something from outside this earth, and this acts as alcohol. And we therefore really only gain insight into things by considering the human being both inside the human being and in the world of nature outside.

This brings me to something quite different, something to add now, in these last minutes, concerning Mr Burle's question about clothes. You see, I have told you all sorts of things about clothes, but it is of course interesting that clothing has really evolved out of human instinct so as to be right for the whole nature of the human being. People have three aspects even as physical beings. They have a head, chest organs, where breathing and circulation mainly take place, inner movement, therefore, and they have outer movement in their limbs. In their physical bodies, therefore, people have three parts: the head, the chest system — I always call it the rhythmic system, because everything moves in rhythm — and the external movement of organs, the outer organization of movement.

Now, you see, in the head it is above all the ether body which is active, in the chest, in the blood circulation and the breathing the astral body, and in voluntary movements the I. If you look at all the clothes that are worn, with the exception of some that are excessively simple, among the savages — you know, real savages — you will always see, whatever fiddle-faddle there may be, that clothing essentially consists of three pieces, somehow or other three pieces. Of course, it is always changed a bit; you just have to consider that in the course of history it has changed terribly. Fiddle-faddle has been added, wishy-washy stuff has been added, but essentially all clothing is in three parts. One has developed from the loincloth or apron. In ancient Egypt men would basically only wear aprons. What is the clothing for that people wear? For the limbs. People showed that they could walk on their feet by covering their feet. The energy of the feet, of the movement organization, was meant to be given expression in the apron.

It is interesting that such things are then passed on, and that Freemasons wear an apron as a special distinguishing mark at their gatherings. That is an ancient Egyptian heirloom. Just as people, at least mostly, have no idea why they wear medals, so they have no idea why they wear an apron. The apron is worn as a sign that one is to be particularly active in one's limbs. And from the apron has evolved anything connected with the limbs, our trousers, for example, but so changed that they prevent rather than help us with walking. So that is the situation with the limbs. The Egyptians made their aprons particularly so that they fitted the limbs; they then put their arms through, and so an apron developed with a part that also covered the front of the chest, and sleeves, so that the upper limbs were also held in it.

The second part, gentlemen, was that people also gave expression to the chest system in their clothing. And this system is best given expression in anything like a shift that is pulled on over the head. This was especially developed among the ancient Assyrians. They evolved the shiftlike garment you put your head and arms through and which then hangs straight down. This gave expression to the chest system, with movement internal. That is also why the folds went like that. The Greeks then took this over as it came across from Asia, and added the artistic folds, imitating the way the main blood vessels run. The way it was done was to imitate the most important part of the circulation and flow in there.

The third thing is the coat or cloak. Originally the cloak was thrown not only over the shoulders but also over the head. You can still see this in some areas, where people still do it like that. The cloak is thrown over the head so that it also covers the head. In throwing on the cloak everything coming from the head was given expression. In the apron more the will that lives in the limbs, in the shiftlike element — you know we still have a little of this in our waistcoats, but you still see it well developed in a priest's garments, the garment of a Roman Catholic priest — and it is still part of female clothing, the garment for the chest. And the head garment is the cloak. It has gone through changes, of course. Think of a cloak thrown over the shoulders and also the head (Fig. 18). Originally it covered the head. If it is a red cloak it is very beautiful. The red colour is such that one would not seek to distort it. Then came the time of which I spoke the last time, when people no longer paid heed to the colours. They then also made themselves black cloaks or blue ones. And what did they do? They cut it off here and made a separate head covering. It became a hat. One can no longer see that today, but I really have to say that when I see someone coming who is wearing a tail coat and top hat I always say to myself: 'Goodness, how you've changed!' For the tail coat and top hat were a single cloak initially. Then the cloak was cut down, given the horrible form of a tail coat, and up above you still have the top hat to cover the head. Think of top hat and tails and try to cut the hat open in front so that you can cast the whole over your head, and you have the garment from which top hat and tails have evolved. One must therefore go back to the old garments and then one sees where our garments come from; although I do not believe Mr Burle wears top hat and tails so often that this would be the reason why he asked the

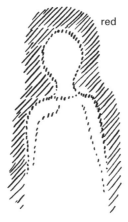

Fig. 18

question (*laughter*). But it does look like it, as if the head itself had been cut off, when people walk around in top hat and tails.

We'll continue next Wednesday at nine in the morning.

Connection between higher aspects of the human being and the physical body. Actions of opium and alcohol

Good morning, gentlemen. Perhaps you have a question again for today?

Mr Müller asked what might cause changes to occur in the pupils.

Rudolf Steiner: That is a very personal question. You'd have to come down to the Institute of Clinical Medicine; I'll tell you when I go there again, so that you may then go there. It is a medical matter.

Another question: *What do the long stripes down the sides of fishes mean?*

Another question: *A man drank a terrible lot of alcohol. He died eight weeks ago. In the last days before he died he ate chocolate and sugar, which he'd never done in his life. How did that happen?*

Rudolf Steiner: Well, with regard to the stripes down the sides of fishes you have to be clear about the following. If one looks at any life form, be it from the plant or the animal world, one has to ask oneself how they relate to the outside world. You see, plants have their green colour first of all in the leaves. This green colour of the leaves comes from a specific relationship which the plant has to light and heat. On one hand a plant takes in what comes from the light and gives other things back, does not take them in. And that is where the green colour comes from.

In the same way you may ask yourself: where does one thing or another come from in fishes? Let me just draw your attention to the fact that fish living in more murky water have a much darker colouring than those that live in light-filled water. Fish that seek out the dark more are bluish, even black. Fish that go more into light-filled water are also lighter in colour. So we can see how external light and warmth influence the fish.

And now consider other animals that live in areas where there is a lot of snow, polar bears, for instance. They take on the white colour themselves. Everything that lives is exposed to the environment in one way or another.

With fish, we see a quite definite relationship between their own essential nature and their environment. The stripes down the side exist to make them subtly sensitive to the light and warmth in their environment. Fish are thus made particularly sensitive. It is not much use for the way they move through the water, but rather for the way they process light and warmth inside. It is therefore a kind of nerve organ.

As to your question concerning the man who drank alcohol all his life and began to be utterly sensible as his end approached, eating sensible chocolate and sugar—you say the last days before his death—this is something we can easily understand if we compare it with countless other such phenomena in life. I have known many people who grew old. As they grew old their handwriting, for instance, became more and more shaky. The writing grew shaky; they were no longer able to write so well, and one could see especially from their handwriting that they had grown old. Earlier they had a handwriting that made them write, let us say, Lehfeld like this [clearly], and then they would write Lehfeld [shakily]. But for the last days before their death it was found that they could write very well again. I have known many people who regained their clear handwriting before their death. It has also been noted in countless cases (this is not in fact my own observation, but these are observations that have been well substantiated) that people who learned a particular language as children—they may have been in a foreign country as children, perhaps, learning a language which they then forgot again (this does happen), let us assume a man of 40 or 50 had had no opportunity to communicate with anyone in this language—would suddenly begin to talk quite comprehensively in this language a few days before their death. It came out again! Now, you see, these are highly significant phenomena. What was really going on? What went on was that a human being leaves his physical body, one aspect of his essential nature, behind for the earth when he dies; it dissolves in the soil, is destroyed in the soil. I have told you that the next aspect, the ether body, gradually dissolves in the general cosmic ether a few days after death. And the human astral body and I are the aspects that remain and go through the world of the spirit. They then go through the world of the spirit.

There, of course, the individual aspects of the human being go through complete separation. And someone with an eye for such things can observe how the different aspects—physical body, ether body, astral body—separate even as death approaches. So what is it when someone changes his handwriting a few days before his death? Well, gentlemen, we do not write with the physical body. What do we actually write with? We write with the I. We only use the physical body as a tool for the I when we write. And our I does not grow old. In your I you are as young today as the day you were born. The astral body also does not grow old to the extent the physical body does. But it is the physical body we have to use as a tool if we want to write. The physical body therefore must take hold of the pen with its hand. When a person gets old, he grows weaker and weaker and is no longer able to get at his physical body properly. What is more, all kinds of things get deposited in the physical body. And the result is that a person can no longer use his fingers so well. He gets clumsy, shaky, instead of making firm strokes in his writing. When the person is close to death, the ether body is beginning to loosen from the physical body. A loosening happens. This may sometimes happen a few days before death; sometimes it happens at the last moment. It would be wrong to say that one should not try to cure a person when days before his death one can see that he may indeed die. Things that have loosened can be put together again. For as long as a person lives we must under all circumstances try to cure them. But it is true, nevertheless, that in many people the ether body loosens days before death comes.

When the ether body loosens the person grows stronger. You can also see this from something else. There are some mad people who develop extraordinary physical strength, tremendous strength. You will often be amazed about the strength such a mad person can develop. Not only is the beating he gives someone much more powerful than that given by someone else, but a mad person may lift pieces of furniture which no one else would dream of lifting with the greatest of ease. So you see, something strange occurs that distinguishes such a person from a normal person. What happens in a mad person? Well, the ether body is always slightly loose in a mad person, or the astral body has loosened. People are not exactly strong in their physical bodies; they are weak. They have to make the ether or the astral body serve the physical body. The popular phrase 'He's got a screw loose' is quite right; something has loosened. Ordinary people often say things that are exactly right, because they have an instinct for the supersensible, and such old saws should not be taken as derogatory but as something that is perfectly true. When a mad person has loosened his ether or astral body and grown strong because of this, he is, as a mad person, in the same situation as someone whose ether body has loosened because he will be dying in a few days' time. And if such a person gets stronger in the ether body he'll be able to write better again. If he gets stronger in the astral body — everything we have forgotten is inside it — he extracts forgotten things from the astral body and is able to speak a language again that he used to know.

But let us take the case you have given. You see, I did not know the man and therefore do not know how he lived. Perhaps you knew him? In that case you'll be able to answer certain questions. Did you know him well? Now you see with such a person it matters a great deal if there was perhaps a woman or someone else about, it may even have been yourself, who was always telling him how bad it is to drink such a lot. (Affirmative.) Well, that will put us on the right track. He has had people around him who always told him not to drink so much, because it was not a good thing and he would do harm to himself. This went in one ear and out the other, as one says. Another popular phrase that has some foundation in fact. It is indeed the case that people's attitude to some things is such that they go in one ear and out the other. Why? Because the astral body does not hear them. The ear is only the instrument of hearing. The astral body fails to hear it.

It may also happen that the astral body hears the thing, but the physical body does not get involved, being too weak. Now consider this. The man has heard Mr Erbsmehl himself say, perhaps: 'You're mad' — I am putting it very strongly, all right? — 'getting drunk all the time. It will not do. It is not the proper thing to do,' and so on. And the man has swallowed it all. That is how it went, for it happens in life that people swallow things and then carry on. But his astral body has held on to some of it. You may have put it so strongly and so often that the astral body and the ether body could not fail to take it in. For as long as they were in the physical body with nothing to hinder them they did not hear. The moment the physical body changed so that the ether body and the astral body became loosened, well, then the idea suddenly came to the person, through the ether body and the astral body: Mr Erbsmehl may have been right after all! Perhaps it is a crazy thing to have done, to drink so much all my life. So now I'll make amends—you can imagine this might happen when things have loosened up. And then the astral body and the ether body say: Ah, now he is no longer drinking alcohol; now he drinks chocolate and sugar water! Of course he might also have had lemonade if there had been any.

The fact that such things may happen proves to someone who takes a sensible view that there may be all kinds of things in a person that do not emerge. I have also told you about the opposite situation before. The opposite case was this. It happened one day to a gentleman of my acquaintance—he was a very learned gentleman—that he lost his awareness and memory. He no longer knew who he was, what he had been doing; he no longer knew any of the learned things he had known. He had forgotten it all. He even did not know that he himself existed. But his intellect was clear. It functioned perfectly. He went to the station, bought a ticket and went far away. He had also taken money with him, money he happened to have on him. He was able to go a long way. When he had arrived at the destination on his ticket he would buy another one, and he did this several times, not knowing what he was doing. The intellect is so much apart from the actual human being that everything was done perfectly sensibly—animals act sensibly, I have given you many examples of this, though they do not have an intellect. One day he found himself again, his memory returned. He knew who he was. His learned knowledge also came back to his head, but he was in Berlin in a hostel for the homeless. That was where he had ended up. He had set out from Stuttgart. It was later possible to establish that he had started from there. In his unconscious state he had been in Budapest and so on. He was able to go back from Berlin to Stuttgart where he was met by a member of his family who had been extremely worried. He was able to function again. He did, however, kill himself later on. One time he got out of it by being unconscious, the other time by committing suicide.

But what is going on in such a case? Well, you see, the man I have told you of stands so clearly before me that I could actually paint him any time I wanted to. He had eyes that made one think they wanted to get more and more deeply back into the head. Here in front he had something that was as if his nose had dug itself in in his physical body — just a hint of all this, of course. He would speak to people in a very strange way. The way he would talk was as if he was convinced in a very different way by his words than anyone else. One had the feeling that he always tasted his words on his tongue and would then swallow them, for he liked them so much. It would please him so much when he spoke that he would swallow it all down. And if anyone contradicted him he'd get really angry. But he would not show much of his anger on the surface, he'd just make a face. He'd startle terribly if a car made a sharp noise in the street, also if you told him anything new. He'd startle irrespective of whether it was good or bad news.

You see, this person had listened too much, and everything immediately left its mark on his physical body. Because of this he had the habit that the astral body would always dig itself in very deeply in the physical body. He did not keep things to himself, the way your alcoholic did, but everything dug itself in deeply in the physical body, until the physical body reached the point where for a time he also shifted his own I out of place.

So there you have the opposite case. In this alcoholic the admonishments remained in the astral body and came out when he loosened up. In this other person, of whom I've told you, the astral body entered so deeply into the physical body, that the physical body then also went away on its own.

You see, the signs are there, everywhere in the human being, that these higher aspects, the supersensible aspects, are closely bound up with his physical body and with his ether body. All this shows, however, that one can really only know life if one looks at life situations that actually tell us: there is a physical body in the human being; there is an ether body in the human being; there is an astral body; there is an I.

You can also see other situations where the person concerned suddenly gets completely new appetites under the moral pressure of what he has left in the astral body during life. There is the following interesting story, for instance, which I'll tell you.[16] A woman was selling vegetables and such things. This was quite some time ago. She would go from door to door with her basket of vegetables. Now she always was the way people would take her to be, looking at life the way a vegetable seller does. She would laugh when someone said something funny; otherwise she was indifferent in life. She brought her vegetables to the door, took her money, and that was how her life went. One day she came to someone's home wanting to sell her vegetables. No one was in except the master of the house, who opened the door. This gentlemen had rather a strange way of looking at people. He would look at them severely and had noted on a number of occasions that when he looked at people in this special way they would get quite talkative about something they did not normally speak of. Now the following happened. It is well documented. The vegetable seller came to the man; he looked at her. She got a shock. He did not say anything, but merely looked at her. He saw she'd been taken aback, but did not say a word and went on looking at her. Then she was not just taken aback but said: 'Don't look at me like that. Please don't look at me like that. I'll tell you everything!' He said nothing and went on looking at her. Then the woman said: 'Yes, but I only did it because I was afraid.' Again he said nothing, but went on looking at her. 'Don't look at me like that! Honest, I would not have done it except that I was afraid.' Again he said nothing, just went on looking. 'I'll tell you everything, but don't look at me like that!' He looked at her. 'I'll tell you everything! You see I would not have murdered it; I only did it because I was scared.' He went on looking. 'You see, I was so afraid of the people; the child would have said something really bad about me, and so I did it out of fear. I didn't really know what I was doing!' And you see, the woman told him the whole story of the murder she had committed on a child. So what had happened there?

The thing is like this. The man had quite a piercing look. When people have the usual kind of eyes, they talk to people but do not really impinge on them that much. When someone's gaze grows fixed and penetrating, then this magnetizes the ether body of a person, as we might put it. And in the ether body is our conscience. When the ether body is properly integrated in the physical body, well, you know, a person will immediately suppress any such things as soon as it rears its head. But if the ether body is magnetized by such a look, it becomes loosened. And when someone has something on his conscience, this also comes loose, rises up and worries the astral body and the I. The result is that people make confessions they would not otherwise make if their ether body has been loosened.

These things show that the ether body, when it is artificially loosened from the physical body, acts independently, and that the physical body really hides a great deal of what people have in them. And when the ether body gets loosened at one's death, the secret may come out—not always, but in a given situation.

Much abuse has been practised with these things. If you were something of an observer of life before the war, you would always see the same if staying at an hotel, or some other place where people collect their letters: some item with the imprint of an American company. It was always the same item. What had happened? Well, an American company had been established and this had branches. One branch was in Berlin, another in Frankfurt; there were such branches in most of the larger cities. Business must have been good, therefore. It was stated that someone wanting to gain power over other people would receive booklets from this American company. He only had to send in so and so much money, and he'd get booklets, and in those booklets he would find directions as to how to gain power over people. Now all the travellers, the representatives, thought to themselves: 'That's a great thing, to gain power over people. By Jove, we'll sell a lot then, for no one will be able to resist us.' The booklets said right away that the person should focus his eyes not on the eyes of another person, but on the point between the eyes; he should stare fixedly at that point. This would magnetize the other person who would then be under his influence and do what he wanted. Now you know, the travellers in wine and other things all sent for this. And one could see that masses of these letters and things were sent to hotels where such travellers would stay. Most of them did not do better in their business in spite of this; it was the American company that did well. Most did not benefit from it. But it may have served some of them, and they did something a person should never under any circumstances do to someone else, for it is a sin against human freedom. No one should seek to gain that kind of power over others! It may be bad enough if it is a natural gift, as in the case of the man I have told you of, but in that case nature had given him that special look. And it is much less abused in such a case than when someone seeks to learn it. Well, such foolishness came to be much less during the war, and today it has largely gone. But we may well say that we can learn from this how people make use even of spiritual things and the worst of materialists — for most of the people who sent for such things were materialists — will actually turn to the spirit if it is a question of making a profit through the spirit. They do not believe in it, but they turn to the spirit if it is a question of making a profit out of it. I wanted to make you aware of the terrible abuse practised with these things.

Much else also has to be considered. Many people have actually practised the kind of thing these people and such booklets were aiming at, though not to such an extent, and have also got somewhere with it. Maybe you have been at meetings where speakers were speaking. Now, you'll admit that the conviction shown by the speaker's words is not always the only thing, but there is a great deal else that comes from the speaker by way of influence. It is a fact that the most popular speakers are often people who gain an influence over the masses by the wrong means. One sees these things happen in the present time.

It is the case, for instance, that I am writing essays on my own life in *Das Goetheanum*.[17] These essays — some of you may have read them — are intentionally written to tell things in the simplest possible way, in plain words, never making too much of things. Now a critic has already appeared who especially finds fault with this. He says I do not write poetry and truth, like Goethe, but truth of a most sober kind. But yes, that is exactly what I am aiming at! And I do not aim to achieve what such a critic demands. Such a critic has exactly the style which compared to a sober style is a 'sozzled' or intoxicated one. And, you see, this intoxicated style is to be found everywhere today. People are no longer concerned to make an effect with what they say, but use words that will overwhelm others. Here we see the beginnings of the wrong kind of influence. For when someone writes the way I am endeavouring to write, this influences the I, which has its own free will. When one writes in an intoxicated style this influences the astral body, which does not have such freedom but is unfree. It is possible to influence the astral body especially by saying things one knows people want to hear.

People who do not want to convince but persuade others mostly use phrases and words other people like, while someone who wants to say the truth cannot always say things other people will like. At the present time it is actually the case that the truth does not generally please people. You only have to look how someone shapes his sentences and you can see that when the person writes his sentences in such a way that they are logical, one following out of another, he will influence the other person's I, which is free. When he writes his sentences so that he is not being logical, but is above all concerned to write things the other person will like, exciting the other person's desires, drives, instincts and passions, he influences the other person's astral body, which is not free. And it is a characteristic of our time that people talk so much about freedom, and that the greatest sin against freedom comes from public pronouncements in the spoken or written word. It really is the case that the spoken and the written word, the written and the spoken word is generally abused in public pronouncements.

You will therefore understand ordinary situations in life better if you are able to distinguish between I and astral body, seeing that one is influencing the one or the other, and you will also be able to understand such things better where a person begins to get his handwriting back before he dies, or will eat something he has never eaten before because of some moral influence. There you can see how the I is integrated in the physical body and becomes loosened.

Another question. The last time Dr Steiner spoke of arsenic. Now the opium question has become acute in Switzerland. A while ago an article by Dr Usteri on the poppy plant and its connection with opium was published in Das Goetheanum.[18] *Could something be said about opium?*

A further question. About two years ago, Einstein's[19] theory became generally known. Today one hears very little of it. Has it proved correct, or has it also gone down the river?

Rudolf Steiner. Well now, I'd have to talk a very long time about Einstein's theory, for it is difficult to present it briefly. To understand it properly one has to know mathematics. But the strange thing about Einstein's theory was that everyone was talking of it though they did not understand it, merely quoting the experts, for, as I said, it does need some knowledge of mathematics. But in so far as some of it can be understood without mathematics — we won't have time for this today — I'll tell you something of it, so that you can see how on the one hand it is based on truth and on the other is very much in error. People still talk about it. The situation with the public at large is that they will rise to the bait when something is spread about by the papers, but they don't hold on to it. The general public have forgotten it by now, but the university professors whose subject it is are all followers of Einstein now. Einstein's theory is thus much more widespread among scientists than it was years ago. I'll present some of it the next time, in so far as can be done in popular terms. It'll need more time than we have left today. Has anyone got another question?

Question. I would really like to know the difference between alcohol and opium. According to Dr Usteri's article one would assume that poppy juice pulls people upwards, and alcohol downwards.

Rudolf Steiner. You see, gentlemen, there we must ask ourselves: when someone drinks alcohol, which aspect of his nature is affected by this? The I. And this has the blood circulation as its physical tool. People are therefore most strongly influenced by alcohol in something that really is their life, in the blood circulation.

With opium, the situation is that it acts particularly on the astral body, and does so in such a way that the person draws it out of the physical body. And you see, he feels particularly well when he thus withdraws the astral body from the physical body. He gets rid of his physical body for a time, and this feels good to him.

People will easily say, and you'll have heard this: sleep is sweet. But the point is that people cannot really enjoy this sweetness, exactly because they are asleep! They cannot sense this sweetness; they can only have an aftertaste of it. And it is because it is an aftertaste that people will say sleep is sweet. When someone takes poppy juice, opium, he becomes aware of this sweetness, for he is then in his body as though he were asleep; yet he is also awake. This enables him to enjoy the sweetness, and this feels tremendously good to him. It is as if his whole body were full of sugar, a very special sugar—filled all the way with sweetness. But his astral body is also free of the physical body, and because of this he perceives all kinds of things, though not clearly. He does not have the usual kind of dreams but perceives the world of the spirit. He likes this. He is lifted up, as you said, into the world of the spirit. Drinking alcohol on the other hand is to have one's physical body taken hold of completely, right down to the blood. Then the astral body does not get free. Everything is laid claim to even more by the physical body. When people drink alcohol, therefore, they are made wholly subject to the physical body, much more so than normally. And that is the difference. With opium, the element of soul and spirit is liberated, on the one hand enjoying the sweetness in the physical body and on the other going on trips, entering into the world of the spirit in a somewhat chaotic way, but entering into it nevertheless.

And the Orientals gain much of what they say of the world of the spirit—not in the right way, but they do speak of it—from taking opium, hashish and the like.

These are things that can show you once again that such things cannot be understood unless one takes account of the higher aspects of the human being.

We'll continue with this at 9 o'clock next Saturday.

Anabolism and catabolism in the human organism. Significance of secretions

Good morning, gentlemen. Perhaps one or the other of you has thought of something he'd like to ask? Or something about what we have been discussing the other day?

Mr Müller asked if Dr Steiner would perhaps say something on a question he put the other day. There are quacks who look at urine samples to see what ails a person.

Rudolf Steiner. Yes, you did ask about that the other day. I simply forgot the question, or there was no more time to answer it.

Mr Müller also wanted to know about the following. There was a man in the Basle area who got good results with his practice of inspecting the urine and the medicines he gave. What should one think of this?

Rudolf Steiner. Well, concerning this issue of examining the urine I would say the following. Examination of the urine is a practice not limited to quacks and the like, but also plays an important role in the medicine that is considered scientific today. There is, however, a big difference between the way in which medical practitioners do this and the people you are really speaking of — essentially not medically trained people. The reason is this. Examination of the urine has always played an extraordinarily important role in the investigation of diseases, from time immemorial. Only you have to consider the following. If you go back to the old medicine which continued until the eighteenth century — for medicine really was only reformed, going into materialism, in the eighteenth century in Italy — you will find that both the diagnosis of diseases and the principles of cure were entirely different. Modern scientists despise the old medicine, and to some extent that is justifiable, but it is not entirely justifiable. And we need to understand the difference between the old medicine and more modern medicine so that we may see what it really means today. The physicians of old knew very well that the human being is not only the physical body we see with our eyes, touch with our hands, but also a supersensible entity that is present throughout the body, something we have always made quite clear.

You'll discover the differences between the old medicine and more modern medicine if you go a long way back in human life, to the time before birth. I am not speaking of the spiritual life before birth but of the physical aspect, the body of a human being in the womb. In modern medicine and science in general, the essential part of human development in the womb is believed to be the way the egg gradually develops. Initially one just has a fertilized egg. It is a tiny cell that can only be seen under the microscope. This multiplies and a kind of cup shape develops. In about the third week this cup turns up a bit on one side. And in the 6th or 7th week the human being looks rather like a small fish. Then the head develops on one side (Fig. 19). Here the first nerve strands develop; and so it goes on. And modern science seeks to gain insight into the development of human beings and also of animals in this way, by observing one form after another.

Fig. 19

But apart from all this, the human being in the womb is all the time surrounded by a thickish fluid. This thickish fluid is here like this [drawing], and only then do we have the womb all around. This thickish fluid, with all kinds of thickish inclusions, is discharged as the afterbirth when the child is born. It is thought to be waste matter, something of no importance, because everything one gets with a living creature today, that is, everything one gets in such a way that it comes out of it, is considered waste matter.

But that is not the case, for it is like this. Here, in the way the cell multiplies and the physical human body develops, the forces of outer nature are active, while the element of spirit and soul is active in the fluid which is then discharged as the afterbirth. This element of spirit and soul is around the small human body to begin with; it only enters into it later. And we really must look for the spirit in the material that later becomes the afterbirth. This is very surprising, of course, but it is extraordinarily important.

People are so much against looking into the spiritual aspect today that a friend of mine[20] undertook to investigate the afterbirth in the light of what I have said, to see how it gradually passes the spirit to the embryo itself, to the physical aspect itself. It would be perfectly possible to make a scientific investigation in this area; it fails merely because modern scientists immediately remove everything found around an embryo if one does become available because the mother dies or an operation is necessary—which does not happen very often. One cannot get embryos that make it possible to investigate this. The way things are done today interferes with genuine scientific investigation. Materialism comes in, I would say, even when the development of the human being is studied.

You know that human beings also produce secretions while they are alive. The things they secrete are not exactly popular in the outside world because they do not smell good. Almost all secretions do not smell good. Today all secretions are – quite rightly – regarded as something that needs to be removed, washed off, and so on.

Human secretions are the one you mentioned, urine, in the first place, secretions of sweat, and also the solid excrement, stools, and some others. The nails you cut are of course also secretions. They are solid secretions. Some things that are secreted, on the other hand, are not seen as secretions, though in reality they certainly are secretions.

You see, the eye is often considered to be the noblest human organ. You only have to think how easily an eye is removed. It has almost completely separated out in its cavity. And the fluid in the eye – I have explained it to you – is also a secretion. And secretion also plays a role in the various organs of hearing, of the ear, which can be seen from the production of ear wax, the outermost secretion. We thus have secretions produced everywhere in the human being; on the one hand the human being is built up, on the other he dissolves, secretes.

What follows from this? Recently I told you something that may be helpful in this respect. I told you that people see nerves, the whole brain, as something that is an organ just like any other organs, like the liver or the spleen. This is not true, gentlemen. The brain is a secretion or excretion. The whole brain, I told you, is an excretion! And if you want to compare the brain to anything you should compare it to the intestine, and indeed to the intestinal contents. If you have a piece of intestine, this would be the intestinal wall (Fig. 20, below), and this the intestinal contents. The intestinal wall is wavy like this. In the brain, the nerve, you do not have the wall; it is there, but it is transparent, not visible, and you have only the contents (Fig. 20, above). You may say, quite rightly: 'What is it that fills the brain?' And if you call the intestinal contents muck, you may also say the brain is muck. Scientifically speaking that is perfectly accurate. For

Fig. 20

thinking activity is not a function of the brain but consists in the brain being excreted, secreted out of our thinking. The higher up you go in the human being, the more is the human being excretion.

I have talked to you about the sense-perceptible and the supersensible human being, the human being you see, and the human being who is also part of us whom you do not see. What we see in the human being is something that is continually produced; it comes from the process in which the human being develops. Here he gets the stumps that will be arms (Fig. 19), here the leg stumps. The super-sensible aspects, the astral body and the I, are there to secrete or excrete, they are continually secreting. Only the physical body and the ether are constructive. The astral body and I destroy what has been built up.

When you build a house you want to build it as quickly as possible and live in it for as long as possible. Nature will gradually destroy the house, for otherwise the houses built in ancient India would still be standing today. But only a few of the houses in our area have existed 300 years ago. In human beings, construction and destruction are simulta-neous. Construction comes first. We eat, take in foods that reach the liver where they are transformed. And destruc-tion, secretion, starts at that point. These processes of con-struction and destruction are really the constant activity of a human being. If we were only to construct, we would be dull and dumb. We'd be a whole lot of dumb fellows. In fact we'd not only be dumb fellows but plants walking about mindlessly if we were only involved in construction. The fact that we destroy matter, continually secreting matter in the brain, for instance, and that we have secretory organs such as the glands, is the very reason why we are not dumb fellows but intelligent people, with variations, of course. Mind and spirit depend on destruction, however, not on construction. And this gives our secretions their special importance.

You see, the thing is like this. The process which occurs when the afterbirth is discharged occurs with all forms of destruction in the organism. The spirit is at work as more and more is destroyed around the developing human being. And when the spirit is able to work in the human body itself once it is born, the afterbirth is no longer needed and is then simply cast off. But things are cast off throughout life. They are cast off as intestinal excretions that may be more or less solid or soft; they are cast off in urine, they are cast off in sweat, for example. You can observe the importance of sweat secretion if you ever have a real nightmare. Say you dream someone is after you to kill you or at least give you a real beating. You run away. In your dream you are running, running, running. Suddenly you wake up, and you are drenched in sweat. A process that has gone so far as to produce dream images that make you afraid takes the form of drenching you in sweat. Such sweats are a physical phenomenon that goes hand in hand with your nightmare. Or think of someone with serious lung disease, someone who is not in the terminal stage but whose lung is not all right. The lung cannot breathe properly and becomes compressed. The person suffers greatly from nightmares. He is also drenched in sweat every time he sleeps. And so you have the connection between the secretion of sweat and these mental activities, images that come in one's dreams. This is a situation, gentlemen, where the ether body is active, for a nightmare only develops at the time one wakes up. For we only think the nightmare went on for most of the night. The whole dream happens at the time one wakes up.

We can prove that dreams happen at the time we wake up. Some time ago, when many of you were not present, I told you a characteristic dream which shows that the whole dream only flashes though our mind the moment we wake up. A student is standing at the door to the lecture theatre. Another student comes and jostles him. That is a terrible insult among students, to be jostled like that. The only possible consequence is a duel; there is no other way. So as soon as the other one has jostled him, he looks for a second; the other must also have a second . . . it's a long story which the student dreams, with all arrangements made, and the seconds negotiating, the whole thing. It all seems to take a terribly long time. He dreams that they go out into the woods, take their positions, measuring the distance by walking it. The pistols are loaded — he dreams all this — they take aim, the first shot is heard, and that is when he wakes up! He instantly realizes that he has been restless in his sleep and knocked over a chair; but the chair is still falling as he wakes up. The falling chair has thus made up the whole dream. The whole dream went through his head at that moment; it merely grew in length in his mind. In reality we only dream the moment we wake up. And this is also why those sick people have their nightmares only as they wake up; they sleep, they wake up, and are then drenched in sweat. The ether body is active in this. As we wake of our own accord in the morning our I and astral body, which have been outside the body during the night, return, and this causes us to break out in a sweat. When we sweat, therefore, it is mainly the ether body which makes us spiritual beings, for stones and plants do not dream, which is also why they do not have mind or spirit.

Now to the elimination of urine. You see, people do not notice it as much as the excretion of sweat because sweat cannot do anything but come out, and it then covers the skin. But if the skin had small sacs in it, with the sweat secreted into them, and if a fine skin were to cover this over, then people would not notice it at all. It could be that one had small sacs in the skin. The sweat would go into these, and at certain times — there might be tiny muscles — the skin would be squeezed and the sweat would run out. In the same way as sweat is secreted through ether body activity, urine is secreted through astral body activity. But people do not realize, for instance, that if they have more lively feelings more urine is secreted than if their feelings are not very strong, and this is because the urine is not immediately discharged from the body. You see, it is like this. If someone is full of enthusiasm and goes on being enthusiastic — irrespective of whether this makes him do things or give thought and attention to something — and did not have a urinary bladder, he would have to pass urine all the time in his enthusiasm. That would be a terrible thing. People would not be able to visit a museum unless there were lots of toilets at hand when they looked at paintings and grew enthusiastic! But human nature has made provision for this elimination. It collects in the urinary bladder and can be discharged at intervals. But urine is mainly secreted because of astral body activity. The astral body is present in all parts of the body, and the urine comes from all parts, collects in the kidneys and then goes to the bladder.

Intestinal elimination is above all governed by the I — in animals by the astral body, but in humans by the I. The eliminatory process involves not only the intestines but the whole human being. There is constant elimination in the whole human being. The intestine is merely the apparatus providing an outlet. We are thus able to say that when we consider eliminations, the ether body is active in secreting sweat, the astral body in secreting urine, and the I in the elimination of faecal matter.

If you think about this you'll not consider eliminations to be something of no importance. Let us assume someone's urine is normal. Well, in that case the person's astral body is also functioning normally. But whether a person is healthy or sick depends on how the astral body is working. Everything in health and illness basically depends on the way the astral body works.

If we eat eggs, for instance, and the eggs are to be digested, the egg must first of all enter the mouth, then the stomach; it then goes into the intestines and there its egg-nature is completely destroyed. The protein is destroyed. But the destroyed protein is rebuilt as it goes to the liver. Human protein develops from animal and vegetable protein on the way from the intestine to the liver. And only human protein then enters the blood.

If you look at the human organism, you have the dia-phragm here (Fig. 21); here is the liver, and here the heart—

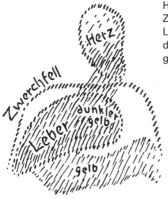

Herz = heart
Zwerchfell = diaphragm
Leber = liver
dunkler gelb = darker yellow
gelb = yellow

Fig. 21

they are only separated by the diaphragm. Material reaching the liver from the intestine is transformed from animal and vegetable protein — I'll make it yellow — into human protein (darker yellow). It is held together in the liver and then passes on into the heart.

The situation is like this. When we eat protein the astral body must work on it, so that animal and vegetable protein is transformed into human protein. If the astral body is lazy, if it cannot work well, the animal protein is not converted to human protein in the liver but goes directly to the kidney and is eliminated in the urine. If we then examine the urine — this is also done in modern scientific medicine — protein is found in it.

Or imagine you are eating potatoes, gentlemen. The potato is largely converted in the mouth, for starch is altogether an important food and exists not only to starch your shirts. Potato consists almost entirely of starch. On the way from mouth to stomach and intestines the potato is gradually converted to sugar. Potato starch first becomes dextrin and then sugar. Potatoes are only bad in the mouth;[21] in the intestines they are uncommonly sweet, for there they are converted to sugar. But when the potato starch has been converted to sugar in the intestine, and the liver has converted potato sugar or any other sugar to human sugar, it gives this inner sugar to the body as a whole, which then grows warmer, gaining inner warmth from it. Again the astral body must function properly if this is to happen. If it does not function properly, the animal and above all the vegetable sugar will not be transformed properly into human sugar but go directly to the kidney. There the sugar is eliminated and the person develops diabetes. The sugar content of the urine will tell you that the person is sick.

All these things are also done in modern medicine, and considered extraordinarily important. In fact, the first thing they do nowadays is to check the urine for protein and sugar. This immediately gives an indication if the person has perhaps one disease or another.

Or take the following. You see, if we want to have a healthy head, and after all this is not entirely unimportant for physical human beings here on earth—people want the head to be healthy, for they believe it to be the most important human organ, so they want to have the head healthy—if we want to have the head healthy, we must bring a substance that is continually produced in us, oxalic acid, through the chest up into the head. A healthy head must have a certain amount of oxalic acid. We produce the oxalic acid ourselves, just as we produce the alcohol we need. But the head has to work properly in turn, so that oxalic acid may be produced. If it does not work properly and the acid remains below, we get a head that is anaemic, and the oxalic acid is taken up into the urine and discharged.

So you see, gentlemen, that even today, a completely ordinary chemical analysis of the urine indicates the most important diseases. But the chemistry we have today did not exist in the past. Medicine did however exist in times gone by.

The situation is like this. Let us assume someone has a temperature—I'll take a drastic situation. What does it mean when we say someone has a temperature? It does not mean that his astral body has grown weak and slack, but that it is excessively active, acting right up into the I. The I is stirred up by this, as it were, if the astral body is excessively active. But the I brings about the blood circulation. And an excessively active astral body, wanting to get into the organs everywhere and being unable to do so, so that it boils up in itself like an ocean whipped up by gales, produces a fever in itself. What will happen next? The blood is made to run too fast in the body. It does not go through its proper transformation. The blood does not have time to develop the organs, but goes from heart to kidney as blood and from there into the urine, and we get a urine that is very dark in colour. Someone able to judge the dark colour of the urine will know that whichever it may be — if it is a little bit darker or very dark — fever is flooding the human organism.

Let us assume the astral body grows utterly indolent, and no longer works properly. Then the blood moves sluggishly in the body, the pulse is barely noticeable. One is able to tell from feeling the pulse how slowly the blood is moving everywhere. Everything gets stuffed up in the body. Pain develops in all kinds of places; the urine turns pale yellow or even white. Now there are all kinds of shades between dark urine and white urine. If someone trains himself to recognize the different shades and takes some urine and looks at it against the light, he can indeed read all kinds of things from the colours of the urine.

The blood continually seeks to replace substance that is lost from the organs. It therefore always has a tendency to turn solid. When the blood rushes through the organs at an excessive pace it cannot give anything to the organs. But it wants to be solid. When it then comes from the kidneys as urine, the urine will be cloudy with that kind of blood. If the astral body becomes sluggish and the pulse weak, one does not have cloudy urine but urine that is almost as clear as water and pure.

So it is not only from the colour but also the cloudiness or clarity of urine that we can draw many conclusions. If the urine looks like a thundery day in summer, with dark clouds, as we look through it, and all kinds of things appear in it, and all is aboil in it, as on a stormy summer's day, then the person has something that creates a high temperature. And if one is able to judge the situation it is possible to tell what disease it is. If the urine looks delightfully clear, like a bright summer's day, with the sun illuminating everything, we may conclude that the person's sickness goes in the opposite direction and he easily tends to have all kinds of organs perish; one organ ceases to function, another organ ceases to function, and so on.

So you see, the situation is such that someone who has trained himself to know the substances eliminated in the urine is able to say a great deal from looking at urine. But that is indeed the difference between the modern medicine we have today and the earlier medicine. In the earlier medicine, people would look at the urine the way we look at a clear or a storm-tossed summer's day, forming more of a rough-and-ready opinion. But having trained themselves, they would base their judgement on the situation as they found it. Modern medicine is highly materialistic and urine is chemically analysed, finding protein, oxalic acid, sugar and so on in it. The difference is therefore that the one would do it more from direct perception, the way it presented itself, and the other does it more by using chemistry.

Now of course it is like this. In earlier times, when people still took this direct inspection seriously, they would learn how to do it properly; they were not quacks. Today most of the people who do it are quacks; though I am not saying they are all quacks. Someone can train himself so well that he can indeed see a great deal, all kinds of diseases. That is a matter of individual training; it needs a great deal of experience and one must make use of that experience.

The difference is this. People do not think much of the spirit today. The spirit is on the point of being got rid of. Anyone can learn what chemistry has to offer. To make a chemical analysis of a substance is easily learned in the three, four, five or six years at university. Basically any fool can make a chemical analysis. And that is indeed the aim. The spirit is to be got rid of. Everyone should be able to do the same. That was not the case in earlier times. Then the spirit was highly regarded. But you have to have spirit to be able to see things in urine. That is the difference. In the past, people were made spiritual by teaching them; today they are made into handymen. It is like this. You need hands if you want to work, and the hands should be guided by mind and spirit. We talk a lot today about people working with their hands or with their heads, doing mental work, but such a distinction should not be made. Someone who works with his hands should also be given the opportunity to develop his mind and spirit, so that he can get to the spirit just as well as someone said to be doing mental work. Differences can only be made between people if we come to appreciate truly spiritual work again. But people want to get rid of the spirit today.

Well, gentlemen, you see from this that in earlier times it was more important in medicine to look at things directly. This also had another consequence. I don't know if you know that today's scientific medical people are rather stuck-up, looking down on the 'muck pharmacy' of old because medicines were made from all kinds of strange things in the past. People would say to themselves: 'Human beings eliminate secretions. If these are brought back into the body again in the right way, they'll immediately want to come out again. And what do they do in that case? They get a sluggish astral body to function in a more regular way again, or a sluggish ether body to function in a more regular way again.'

Now you'll say: 'If one finds that someone's astral body has grown sluggish, one might give him sweat as a medicine.' You might say this. And you might say: 'Well, that's the old muck pharmacy, for that really had something of this.' Well, there is in fact no great difference. For if you were to investigate the products used for medicines today you would find that they are the same products as are found in sweat, only they are put together from outside, out of mineral substances. The ancients used the actual sweat.

And it was in many respects more effective than the things one puts together, for—as I have told you on many occasions—nature is much cleverer than people are. People can combine things to make medicines which nature combines herself. It was a strange thing, but the ancients appreciated something that is not at all appreciated today. The ancients would say: 'When someone gets up a good sweat, he has a blanket of sweat all around him' (Fig. 22). So that is the first thing. But people secrete sweat all over their body surface. If we could leave this sweat which the person secretes and take away the person, just think, it would be like this. Here someone is sweating terribly; the whole body surface is covered with sweat. Now imagine I could take the person away and the sweat would stay where it was. That would leave an impression of the whole person; we would have the whole person in the sweat! Most interesting, is it not? The situation is that sweat all the time seeks to reproduce the human form.

Fig. 22

The ancients also did something else. Not only did they look at sweat in this way, but they also looked at urine like this. So they would have a small glass of urine, for example (Fig. 23). They were still able to see things better in the spirit; and lo and behold, something like a spectre of the person would arise from the urine for them. Something the sweat created by itself, being on the surface, was rising up, as it were, from the urine. People really saw that in the past, if they had a vial of urine. So there arose—I don't know if you know the story of Venus, the goddess, rising from the sea foam—that is how a human astral spectre would rise from the urine. And when someone tended towards a particular illness, let us say, consumption, the astral spectre would be thin and dried up. When someone tended to be unnaturally fat, the spectre would be swelling up on all sides. You may call it fanciful that someone should see a different spectre arising from light-coloured urine than

Fig. 23

from dark urine. But they did see it. And as physicians of old they would judge diseases in this way.

And the same thing happened at the time when people studied not only the urine but also the faecal matter passed as stools. These were particularly important in the past for determining diseases. Just imagine someone taking a look at the stools. One will find that the stools of one person contained much sulphur, those of another person much iron. Depending on what is in there, you may have more sulphurous intestinal contents. Dogs, for example, have much sulphur in their intestinal contents and this then goes outside. The more sulphur it contains, the more whitish and firm the faecal matter. The more carbon, carbon-type matter there is in it, the darker is the intestinal content; cats have this. It is therefore possible to conclude what illnesses people have by looking at the faecal matter passed as stools, much better even than from urine.

With faecal matter the ancients also had a vision; it was in their nature to have such visions. This is something quite remarkable. They would say that when someone secreted sweat he enveloped himself in his own spectre. And when someone passed urine a spectre would rise from it. The situation with intestinal contents is that they have boundaries all round and distinct colours. And in ancient times diseases were widely diagnosed according to those visions, or dreams, if you like.

Today people will imitate this rather inaccurately, sometimes in a very silly way. They read it up in ancient tomes which we can hardly understand today. There are some who will diagnose illnesses from the stools, but usually this will not get them very far. But someone may gain considerable experience in this, and then it could prove fruitful. Modern scientists do not think much of this, however, for they prefer to use chemical analysis for everything. But, as I said, examination of the urine is as important in medical science today as it is in the unscientific medicine that is something left over from earlier times.

Looking through ancient medical books you will come across a term which you'll not normally be able to understand. All kinds of mystics and people who fancy they have the whole of wisdom, not only knowledge but wisdom, will keep telling you what they have read in those ancient tomes. It does not mean much, for they do not understand those old books. But if you read them yourselves you'll find a particular term. Again and again you'll see the term 'mummy'. The books will say: if the 'mummy' is clear and bright, the person will be afflicted with all kinds of conditions that drive him to consumption and so on; if the 'mummy' is very dark, blackish, the person will have a fever, heated diseases. The books always speak of how the 'mummy' is, and diagnose diseases by this.

What is this 'mummy'? People reading this today know only of Egyptian mummies. So what do they actually make of it if they read that the 'mummy' is bright or dark? They'll never know what is meant by this. But what did the people who wrote those ancient medical books mean? The form that is produced in sweat, the form that arose from the vial of urine and from the stools — that is what they called the 'mummy'. The mummy was in fact the spiritual human being. And the spiritual human being became visible through the eliminations. The ancients would say: when a child is born, the afterbirth is discharged, and with this the last remnant of the spiritual human being goes away. If people were to investigate this today they would find that when a little child is born it is sometimes only very little which is discharged as afterbirth, and therefore very little that is supersensible. But there are others where a great deal is discharged. These people, where a great deal is discharged — the spirit departs even as they are born — later become materialists.

And that is how it is, gentlemen. Spiritual activity in the human being, astral and I activity, has extraordinarily much to do with secretion and elimination. When people spoke of the old muck pharmacy, this shows they no longer appreciated what used to be appreciated in the past. Waste phenomena are no longer appreciated today. In many ways it is of course a good thing if they are not given too much appreciation, for that may lead to all kinds of things. I once knew someone who wanted to stop washing, for having heard that the spirit lives in our eliminations he said we should keep our eliminations, including the dirt. And the result was that he had a great appreciation for dirt! Well, gentlemen, that may sometimes seem foolish. But it is not always foolish.

Take horses, for instance. You know they have hoofs down below, and there is a transition from the hoof to the soft part of the horse's toe. Dirt collects in that part. And it may happen that a horse gets sick if you keep scraping off that dirt. You need an instinct to tell you for how long the dirt should be left, so that the horse can keep up with producing this dirt. But there in the horse it is perfectly easy to see the importance of the dirt, the elimination. In humans the matter is important for their spiritual aspect, including health and illness. And the ancients called the spiritual aspect of the eliminations the 'mummy'. If you find the word 'mummy' in old books from now on you'll know what it means, for I have told you how the 'mummy' develops from the products of elimination.

You see, there is a vast science in the question Mr Müller asked, but a science we can only cope with if we consider the spiritual aspect. Otherwise everything that is eliminated is simply a product of elimination; one takes no heed of it. But people show by their eliminations what kind of spirit lives in them. And you need only take a superficial look to see this in the case of faecal matter. Compare horse dung with cow dung. Cow dung is larger, and it spreads. Horse dung consists of what are almost little round heads. If you have a feeling for beauty you cannot help but say, as you see a cow pat: 'The whole cow!' There we have its image, with its broad gait, its leisured activity, its inclination to lie down; the whole cow is there in that cow pat. And the horse, the jumping jack of the animal world, always wanting to come away from the earth, wanting to leap and jump away and out into the world — horse droppings reveal the whole horse! And that is how it is with the faecal matter of animals; one can see the whole animal in it. So you can see what the ancients meant by a 'mummy', and that it was simply astral. The supersensible animal, the supersensible human being, lives in the eliminations.

We can cope with these things if we have the science of the spirit. Now of course, this should not cause our enemies to say that the science of the spirit concerns itself with sweat, urine and so on, and is therefore really a muck science. This would suit our enemies only too well!

And so, gentlemen, because you have asked the question I had to show you the truth of it. But you may also point out, whenever the opportunity arises, that it is not a matter of studying something that is muck, but of studying the spiritual element. For a person will faint if the constructive principle is too powerful in him. Tumours will develop if he only constructs. He must also destroy, doing so in the right way. He will faint, be permanently insensible and not there in the spirit if a tumour develops in the brain, for in that case only construction takes place. The tumour develops when destruction is not playing its role in the brain. And the nerves of the brain are products of destruction, spiritual products of destruction. But if the process gets too powerful, then the blood comes in too strongly and inflammation develops. And there you have the difference between tumours and inflammation. If your urine is dark, you have a tendency to inflammation somewhere in the body. If your urine is light coloured, you tend to develop tumours. This is one thing. But you can diagnose all diseases in the urine, if you know how to examine it properly.

We'll continue on Wednesday.

Einstein's theory of relativity. Thinking divorced from reality

Good morning, gentlemen. Has anyone thought of something for today?

Mr Burle asked about the theory of relativity and what the situation was today. One read a lot about it, especially earlier. Now it had perhaps been forgotten again; at least one no longer heard so much about it.

Rudolf Steiner. Well, you see, the situation with the theory of relativity is a difficult one, and so you'll probably have to pay careful attention today and in the end you'll still say, even if you did pay good attention, that you do not know it. But it is the same for many people who talk about the theory of relativity today. They talk about it, often praising it as the greatest achievement of our age, but they do not understand it. I'll try and speak of it in as popular a way as possible. As I said, it will be difficult today, but I am sure we'll get back to more interesting things the next time.

Einstein's theory refers to the movements of any body. You know that bodies move by changing their position in space. To draw a movement we say: a body is in a position *a* and moves to another which we may call *b*. So if you see a railway train go past, standing somewhere outside, you will at first be in no doubt but that the train is rushing past you, that it is moving and you are standing still. But doubts may arise quite easily, for the moment of course only if you do not give it any more thought, if you are sitting in a railway carriage and are asleep at first, then wake up and look out of the window. A train is going past. You have the distinct feeling that a train is going past. This need not be true, however, for before you went to sleep your train was stationary, and while you were asleep your train started to move. You did not notice, being asleep, that your train started to move, and it seems that the other train is moving past. If you take a closer look you find that the train outside is stationary, but your train is moving. So you are in motion but believe you are at rest and the other train is in motion, when in reality it is at rest. You know it can also happen that you look out of the window and believe yourself to be at rest in the train you are in, and the whole train is going in the opposite direction. That is what the eye perceives. And so you see that the things we say about movement are not always correct. You wake up and form the opinion that the train outside is in motion. But you immediately have to correct yourself: Hey, that is not true; it is standing still and I am travelling!

It has happened that an opinion had to be corrected in this way on a much larger scale on one or indeed several occasions in world history. We only need to go back six or seven centuries. People then held the view that the earth stood still in space, with the whole of the starry heavens moving past it. This view was corrected in the sixteenth century, as you may have heard. Copernicus[22] came along and said: 'None of this is true. The sun, the fixed stars are in fact standing still, and we with our earth are flying through space at a tremendous speed.' We thought we were at rest on earth—just as the person in the train thought he was at rest and the other train was moving—and we have now corrected this. Copernicus corrected the whole of astronomy, saying it was not true that the stars moved; they stood still, whereas the earth with the human beings on it was rushing through space at a vast speed.

So you can immediately see that we may not always say right away how things are with movement—whether we ourselves are at rest and a body moving past is truly in motion, or we ourselves are moving and a body we think is rushing past is at rest.

I think if you consider this you'll say to yourselves: 'Yes, it may be necessary to make such a correction for anything we recognize to be movement.' But just consider how long it took before the whole of humanity came to make the correction for the movement of the earth. It took thousands of years. When you are sitting in a train it may perhaps only take seconds before you correct your opinion. It therefore varies how long we take to correct such an opinion.

This has made people like Einstein say that we really cannot know if something we see in motion actually is in motion or if we are not in some mysterious way in motion as we stand there motionlessly and the other is in fact motionless; let us therefore draw the final conclusion from this uncertainty.

Well, gentlemen, in that case it might be like this. Let us assume this is a car. You drive the car from Hansi House up to the Goetheanum. But who can say that the car really comes up here? Who can say this with certainty? The car might be completely motionless, only its wheels turning, and the whole of the Goetheanum towards which one is driving might be moving down the hill in the opposite direction. It just needs for something to emerge the way it did emerge for Copernicus in relation to the earth! (*Laughter*)

Einstein took such things and said: 'We can never be certain if it is the one body that moves or the other. All we know is that they move relatively to each other, that the distance between them changes; that is the only thing we know.' Of course we know it when we drive to the Goetheanum, because we come closer to the Goetheanum, but we cannot know if it comes to us or we go to it. Now you see, when we speak of being truly at rest or truly in motion, those are absolutes. What then is absolute rest or absolute motion? It would be a state of rest or a movement of which we could say: 'The body is at rest within the universe or it moves.' But that is an awkward business, for at the time of Copernicus it was still believed that it was the sun that stood still and the earth that moved around it. This is true for the earth, but not for the sun, for the sun is moving very fast, rushing through space at a terrific speed relative to an astral cosmos in the constellation of Hercules — and all of us with it, of course.[23] On the one hand we are orbiting the sun, but as we orbit the sun we rush through cosmic space with it. We thus cannot say that the sun is absolutely at rest in cosmic space. And because of this Einstein and others who held the same views said that we simply cannot be certain that anything is absolutely at rest or in absolute motion; we can only say that things are relatively at rest — relatively meaning in relationship to each other — they appear to us to be at rest or in motion.

You see, gentlemen, there was an occasion during a course given in Stuttgart where someone thought we anthroposophists do not really know anything worth knowing about the theory of relativity, and being a fanatical adherent of that theory he wanted to show people that the theory of relativity really has validity. What did he do? He took a box of matches and said: 'Here's a match. I now hold the box so that it does not move and move the match away from me and towards it. It ignites. Now I make a second experiment. I hold the match so that it does not move and move the box towards me. Again the match ignites. The same thing happens. What has happened is that a flame has been ignited. But the movement I made is not absolute; it is relative. On the one occasion, if that is the box and this the match, I move the match in this direction, and on the other occasion the box. It does not matter if I want to make a fire if the box is moving or the match, but only that they move relative to one another.'

This can be applied to anything in the world. You can say, speaking of the whole world, the situation is that we do not know if one thing moves or another, or one moves more actively and the other less so. All we know is that they move relative to one another, coming closer or going further apart. That is all we know. And we do not know if one body moves faster or more slowly. Let us assume you are in a fast train travelling at speed and a slow train goes past outside. You are looking out of the window. You cannot judge what is really going on, for as you travel in your fast train and the slow train comes along you have the feeling that your fast train is going much more slowly than it did before. Try it. At that moment you have the feeling that the train is suddenly going much more slowly. Your perception is that the speed is reduced by as much as the speed of the train that is coming the other way. So you get completely the wrong idea about the speed at which your train is travelling. If on the other hand a train is travelling next to yours that is going more slowly, you get the feeling that yours is going faster. You can never judge how two movements are relative to each other but only how the distance between them changes.

We may stop at this point and say: 'This Einstein really was a clever fellow, he has finally realized that you cannot speak of absolute movement in the universe but only of relative movements.' It is clever, and, as you will understand, it is true for many things. For no one seeing a star, let us say, at rest can say it is a star at rest. If you move at a certain rate, the star seems to move in the opposite direction—but it may also be moving towards you. So you cannot say from just looking at it if it is at rest or in motion. It is necessary for us to know this; and knowing this, the whole way of putting things in some of the sciences today really ought to change. Let me give you an example of this.

How do we gain knowledge of the stars? You cannot gain

knowledge of the stars if you take the view a certain prince once took who went to an observatory where the astronomer had to show him the observations he was making, of course, him being the ruler of the land. So he let the prince look through the telescope and they observed a star. If you aim a telescope just anywhere you'll not see anything at first. You have to wait a little and then the star will appear and finally disappear again on the other side. The prince looked at this and then he said: 'Right, now I can see you know something about the stars; you know where they are and how they move. I see that. But what I fail to understand is how you can know the names of the stars, seeing they are so far away.' Such views will not get us far in astronomy. But what happens when we observe the stars? We have a telescope, and the astronomer sits there — seeing his head from above — looks into it and there is the reticle here, where two threads cross, and one establishes the location of the star.

In the past, observers always thought one might say: 'Either the earth has moved, or one has moved the telescope on, moving the objective' — that is the objective or lens system, which is further away (the glass that is nearer to one is called the eyepiece) — 'so far that one sees the star at rest in it.' In the old days people thought the star moved. Today we have to say that we do not know anything about the resting or moving state of a star. All we can say is that at that moment the reticle of my telescope coincides with the image of the star. The two coincide. We cannot say more than what is immediately in front of our eyes. We would thus have no certainty about the world as a whole.

This has tremendous implications. It is important when we consider the movements not only of heavenly bodies but also of bodies here on earth. And the consequences drawn by Einstein and others who think like him go a very long way. They said, for instance, that if motion was only relative and not absolute one could never say anything valid about anything, not about things happening at the same time nor about different times. If I have a watch in Dornach, for instance, and another in Zurich, with the hands in the same position, I am far from certain that it may not be true that my observation is wrong, for they are some distance apart. It is possible that there is no such thing as simultaneity, with things happening at the same time.

So you see, enormous consequences were drawn from the matter. And the question is: shall we never be rid of this problem? Is there nothing at all we can say about the things themselves as they are in motion? That is the important question. What is certain is that we cannot say anything about their movements as we look at them. And it is also true in the widest sense that when I drive up to the Goetheanum in a car, it may just as well be that the Goetheanum is coming to meet me.

But there is one thing, gentlemen, that does happen. Even the example of the matchbox which I quoted is not entirely true. For you see, I could have called out to the gentleman who gave such a fine demonstration: 'How about nailing the box to the table and see how well you can move it then! You'd certainly need a lot of strength to move the whole table to and fro.' So there is something not right somewhere.

You can find out what it is if you consider the matter very carefully. Let us assume you go by car from Dornach to Basle. Now we might say it is not true that the car is moving; it is stationary and only the wheels are moving, and Basle is coming to meet it. Fine. But there is one thing that speaks against it. The car will be worn out after some years. And the fact that the car is worn out can only be due to the fact that it was not the road that moved but the car, and that it has been worn out, ruined, by what went on inside it. So if you do not only look at the movement but also inside the body itself to see what effect movement has, then you will realize that Einstein's conclusion does not apply all the way. So you'll find that the car wears itself out, and it is not only that the tyres are worn down from going round and round. Now someone might say: 'Well, they would also go round if the hill were coming towards one, or if Basle came towards one, for otherwise that would get worn down.' And then one might still say: 'Maybe it is like that after all. It is not easy to decide in the case of lifeless bodies.' And all you can say in the case of lifeless bodies is that it is uncertain how much the one or the other is moving. But a living organism! Imagine you walk to Basle, and someone else stays here in Dornach, standing still for the two hours you need to walk to Basle. Now, if you had not moved towards it but Basle had come to meet you, you would have practically done no more than the other person who remained standing still. But you've grown tired. A change has come over you. This change, which is happening inside you, does tell you that you have moved. And with living bodies it is possible, in a way, to tell from the change that happens in them if they are truly in motion or only in apparent motion and therefore at rest.

And that is also what must help us to realize that one must not base theories on observations made in the world, not even something that seems as obvious as movement does. We must base our theory on internal changes. So the situation is that with the theory of relativity, too, we have to say to ourselves: someone who only looks at the outer aspect of things will not get anywhere; you have to consider the inside. And then the theory of relativity actually helps us to make at least a beginning with the science of the spirit, with anthroposophy, for in anthroposophy we are always asked to consider the inner aspect.

Einstein's theory has had some extraordinarily strange consequences. The matter gets particularly interesting, for instance, when Einstein gives examples. One example was his effort to prove that the change in location has no significance at all. He therefore said: 'If I fling a watch the hands of which are in a particular position out into space so that it goes out at the speed of light, turns round and comes back again, this movement has had no significance for the inner parts of the watch. The watch comes back unchanged.' That was the kind of example Einstein would give. 'If a body moves or not — we cannot tell. The watch is the same, it is the same to it if it moves or remains at rest.' But, gentlemen, one simply has to ask you to look at the reality of a watch flying out into cosmic space at the speed of light and coming back again. You won't see anything of that watch. It will have been pulverized so that you can no longer see it.

What does this mean? It means one cannot think like that. It leads to thoughts that are thoughtless. And so you'll find on one hand that Einstein is a very clever man, and that he draws conclusions, forms opinions that people find most attractive. You know, ordinary people who are not the best of mathematicians will not understand much of Einstein's theory. And then they begin to read about Einstein's theory in some popular book. They read the first page and give a yawn; they read half the second page and then they stop. And they'll say: 'It must be something terribly clever. For if it were not terribly clever I would be able to understand it. And a lot of people are saying that it is something very clever.' This is how public opinion has been formed concerning the theory of relativity. But there are people who do understand it. And Einstein's followers come from among those who do understand it, their numbers growing daily. It is not that it has been forgotten, as Mr Burle thinks. University professors did not want to know about Einstein's theory if you tried to talk to them about it a few years ago. Today people in the academic world in particular are full of Einstein's theory.

But people do develop strange notions about it. I once

had a debate about Einstein's theory with university professors. Now, you see, for as long as one stays in the area which I have also been discussing here, Einstein's theory of relativity is correct. There's nothing you can do about it. It is like that with railway trains, with solar systems, with movements in the whole world. In that respect it is quite correct. But the academics then apply it to everything and say, for example: 'The size of a person is also relative. He does not have absolute but only relative size. It merely seems to me that he is that tall. He is that tall in relation — well, seeing we are here — to the chairs or to the trees, but one cannot speak of an absolute height.' Now you see, that holds true for as long as we are only dealing with geometry. The moment we stop dealing with geometry and come to life itself, the situation changes and we are singing a different tune. You see, someone who has no feeling for it can carve a human head that is a hundred times the size of your head. He then has a head. But someone who has a feeling for this would never do this, for he knows that the size of the human head is not relative, for it is determined by the whole of cosmic space. The person may be a little taller or shorter, but when someone is a dwarf that is because of an illness. When someone becomes a giant that, too, is due to illness. It is not just relative, for the absolute nature is already apparent. Human sizes do, of course, vary within limits. But in the universe the human being is destined to have a particular size. So again we cannot speak of relativity. We can only say that a human being gives himself a particular size because of his relationship to the universe. Only one of the group of professors with whom I had the debate would admit this. The others had their minds twisted to such an extent by the theory of relativity that they said the size of a human being, too, is relative, for that is how we look at it.

Now you know that if you have a painting it may be

large; when you walk away it gets smaller and smaller, according to the law of perspective. The size of the painting, you see, is relative. The relativity theoreticians therefore believe that the size of the human being, too, is only the way it is because it is seen against a particular background. But that is nonsense. The size of the human being has a quality of being absolute, and a person cannot be much taller and not much shorter than predetermined.

People think all this up because they have no real idea as to what is involved in a process or an object that is somewhere near us on earth. You will be able to realize from everything I have been saying that if that is the earth, and there is a human being on the earth, you know he depends not only on the forces of the earth but on forces that influence him from beyond the earth. Our head for instance reflects the whole universe. We have spoken of this. If it were of no importance what size a person is, what would have to be then? Let us assume Mr Burle's head, Mr Erbsmehl's head and Mr Müller's head is created out of the universe. Well, gentlemen, if the heads differ in three or four different ways here, then there would have to be an extra universe for each. But there is only one universe, and it does not grow bigger or smaller for the sake of an individual person but is always there, always the same, and because of this human heads must be approximately the same. Only people who do not realize that we all share the same world, which also has spiritual influences, believe it does not matter what size a person's head is and say that it is merely relative. It is not relative but depends on the absolute size of the universe.

So we have to say to ourselves again: it is indeed the case that if one thinks about the theory of relativity in the right way that one comes to the science of the spirit and not to materialistic science.

And if one looks more closely at the human being, one

can see that people who think like Einstein run out of ideas when they come to the sphere of life or of the spirit. You see, as a boy I was able to take part in the lively debates held on the forces of gravity. Gravity — if a body falls to the ground, you say it has weight. It drops because it has weight, gravity. But the force of gravity is active throughout the universe. Bodies are attracted to one another. If this is the earth and this the moon (Fig. 24), the earth attracts the moon and the moon does not fly off like this, but moves in an orbit around the earth because the earth always draws it back to itself just as it is on the point of flying off. When I was a boy people were disputing with one another as to what really causes gravity.

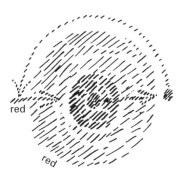

Fig. 24

Newton, the English physicist[24] of whom I have been telling you before, simply said: 'Bodies are mutually attracted.' This is not an entirely materialistic view, for you only have to think what it takes for a person to take hold of something and draw it to him and you can see it needs all kinds of things other than the material. Now if the earth is to attract the moon, one really cannot speak of a materialistic view at all. Yet in my young days materialism was flourishing. We might also say it dried people up, making them wither, but we might also say it flourished. And people would say: 'That is not true; the earth cannot attract the moon, for it does not have hands to draw it to itself. That is not possible.' Then they said: 'The cosmic ether is everywhere (see drawing).' So what I am drawing red here is the cosmic ether; it consists of lots of small grains, tiny little grains. And these tiny little grains bump into here, and bump into there, but bump more there than they do in the middle. So if you have two bodies, earth and moon, and there is more pushing from outside than from the inside, it is as if they were attracted to each other. The force of attraction, of gravity, was therefore explained as pushing from outside.

I cannot describe the painful process I went through to gain insight at that time. I really kept turning the matter over in my mind from my 12th to 18th year – does the earth attract the moon, or is the moon pushed towards the earth. For you see, the reasons people gave were mostly not exactly stupid but clever. But here we already have something of a theory of relativity. One asks oneself: is there something absolute in this or is it all relative? Perhaps it really does not matter if we say the earth attracts the moon, or the moon is pushed towards the earth? Perhaps the issue cannot be decided. You see, people gave the matter a great deal of thought. And what I really want to say is this: they did at least realize at the time that apart from visible matter there is also the ether. They needed the ether, for how could one speak of something that was pushing unless it was those grains in the ether. When Einstein first established his theory of relativity, people still believed in the existence of the ether. And Einstein thought of everything he described as relative motion as being in space, and space being filled with ether. Then he realized: 'Wow! If motion is merely relative, there is no need for there to be any ether. Nothing needs to pull, nothing to push. All this cannot be decided, and so it may also be that space is empty.'

As time went on there really were two Einsteinian theories. It was of course one and the same person. The earlier Einstein described everything in his books as if the whole of cosmic space were filled with ether. Then his theory of relativity made him say: 'Space is empty.' Only with the theory of relativity there is no point in saying anything about the ether, for one simply does not know if it is like that. And some of the examples he gives are indeed grotesque. He says, for example: 'If that is the earth and there is some kind of tree, I climb up the tree; here I slip, and fall down' — it is something you probably all know; I certainly had it happen to me quite often as a boy that when I climbed up a tree and lost my grip I would fall down. And you say: 'The earth is attracting me. I have weight. This is because of the force of gravity, for otherwise I would have remained hanging in the air, I would be waving my arms and legs about if the earth did not attract me.' But Einstein thinks you can't say all this, for imagine the following. There you have the earth again and now I am up there on a tower. But I am not standing in a place where there is open world all around me, for I am in a box, and the box is suspended from above. If I drop off the tower in my box, my relationship to the walls remains the same. I am not aware of being in motion, for the walls come down with me. So now I cannot say if the rope on which my box is suspended is let down from above and I arrive at the bottom in my box because someone is letting me down, or if I get down there, if the box loses its hold, because the earth attracts me. I cannot determine this. I do not know if I am let down or if the earth is attracting me.

But the situation with this example chosen by Einstein is just as it is with the example always given in schools. It is explained to the children how a planetary system develops; that at first there is a nebula, and the planets separate out from this misty nebula. The sun remains at the centre. And people say it is easy to prove that this is true. Take a little drop of oil floating on water, and in the middle a piece of card with a pin stuck through it. You put this into the water, and begin to rotate it. Tiny droplets then split off from the bigger one, and you have a tiny planetary system.[25] And it must be the same out there. Once there was a nebula; the planets split off, and the sun remained at the centre. How could anyone contradict this when they see that drop of fat even today! Well, yes, but one little thing has been over-looked, gentlemen, which is that I have to be there and rotate the pin if I am the teacher showing this to the children. If I do not rotate it, no little planetary system will develop! And so the teacher would have to tell the children that there is a huge teacher out there who once made it turn. Only then would the example be complete. And Einstein, if he were to think in terms of reality—if he ever gets to develop such an idea—would have to assume that someone up there is in charge of the rope. This is equally necessary. Otherwise you cannot say it does not matter how I come down off the tower, whether someone lets me down or I fall down; there must be someone up there. And giving his example Einstein would have to immediately remember to say: 'Who is holding the rope?' But he does not, for the materialism of our present age does not permit him to do so. So he thinks up examples that do not relate to reality, that one cannot think, that are impossible to think.

And there is something else, too. Imagine a hill, gentle-men. There you have the town Freiburg im Breisgau. I set up a cannon on the hill so that you'll be able to hear it in Offenburg, if you like, when it is fired. If someone notes the time when he heard the bang in Freiburg and if someone else has heard it in Offenburg, you get a difference in time. The sound needed some time to get from Freiburg to Offenburg.

Now you see, this business has also been made use of for

the so-called theory of relativity. For people say let us assume I am not in Offenburg and hear the bang but in Freiburg. There I hear it as it happens. I now travel in a train from Freiburg to Offenburg. Moving away from Freiburg, I hear the sound a little later than when it happened. I would hear it still a little later if I were closer to Offenburg, and even more the further I go in that direction.

But this will only happen for as long as you travel more slowly than the sound does. If you travel at the same speed as the sound going from Freiburg to Offenburg, what will happen? If you travel at the same speed as the sound, you arrive at Offenburg and it runs away from you — you still do not hear it. If you travel at the same speed you'll never hear it. You are meant to hear it, but it's gone. Now people will say: Wow, that is right, you don't hear the sound any more when you move at the same speed as the sound. And if you move even faster than the sound, what happens then? If the movement is slower you hear it later; if it goes at the same speed you don't hear it at all. If you move faster you hear it sooner than it happens! And people will say that is quite natural, it is properly thought out. So if you hear the sound two seconds later in Offenburg, moving more slowly than the sound, you do not hear it at all if you move at the same speed as the sound. But if you move faster than the sound you hear it two seconds earlier than the cannon was fired in Freiburg! Now I'd like to invite you to listen, really listen to the sound before it is produced in Freiburg! Try it to convince yourselves; see if you'll hear it sooner, even if you go ever so fast.

The other thing that goes against this is that I would also like to ask you what you'll look like if you move as fast or even faster than sound.

What follows from this? It follows that you can think what you like providing you do not stick to reality. With the theory of relativity, people finally arrive at the idea that you can hear the sound before the cannon is actually fired! (*Laughter*) It is perfectly possible to think these things, but they cannot actually happen. And, you see, that is the difference. People doing scientific work today mainly want to think logically; and Einstein is wonderfully logical in his thinking. But logical is not in itself real. You have to have two qualities in your thinking. In the first place, things certainly have to be logical, but they must also be in accord with reality. You must be able to live in the real world. Then you won't think up a box pulled up and down by a rope. You won't think of a watch flying out into space and back again at the speed of light. Nor will you think of someone moving faster than sound and hearing the sound before the cannon is fired. Many of these ideas presented in books today, gentlemen, are well thought out, but they do not relate to the real world.

We are thus able to say that Einstein's theory of relativity is clever and does hold true for some things in the world, but you cannot do anything with it when you look into reality. For the theory of relativity will never tell you why someone gets extremely tired going to Basle, seeing he is unable to say if he is going to Basle or if Basle is coming to meet him. His tiredness would be inexplicable if Basle were coming to meet him, and why I do things with my feet when I walk. I might simply stand still and wait for Basle to come to me. You see, all this shows clearly that it is not enough to think correctly and cleverly, for there has to be something else. We have to accept the reality of life and decide on things in relation to life.

This is what I am able to tell you about the theory of relativity. It has attracted a great deal of attention, but, as I said, people do not really understand it, otherwise they would reflect on these things.

We'll meet again next Saturday.

Appendix

How the lectures for the workers at the Goetheanum came about*

Viktor Stracke

In the summer of 1920 and up to the time of the first course for university students, Dr jur. Roman Boos would occasionally give us, the work people, conducted tours of the Goetheanum to explain it, lectures given during our paid working hours. This gradually came to an end. It may be that Dr Boos had too much to do, or that his way of speaking was not sufficiently comprehensible for a group that included a number of simple country people and he felt that there was no real response.

There were about 30 or 40 of us at the time, and according to the work we did and the training we had we may be said to have fallen into three groups.

1 Actual building workers under their foreman Mr Schleutermann; a typical member of this group was Mr Gränicher from Gempen. I last met him a few years ago when he was looking after the heating system in the Schreinerei, the last of the workmen from the First Goetheanum still to be working at the Second Goetheanum.

2 The woodwork specialists (cabinet makers) under master cabinet maker Mr Lidvogel (whom we had given the nickname Limvogel = lime bird; he was a brother-in-law

---

* From *Mitteilungen aus der anthroposophischen Arbeit in Deutschland* Nr. 73, Michaeli 1965 S. 184-8. English by A. R. Meuss, FIL, MTA.

of Mr Schleutermann's). People I specially remember from this group are cabinet maker Mr Erbsmehl with his handsome beard (later also his son), who was already livening up his small house in Grellingen with Goetheanum forms, and Mr Sonderegger.

3 The group of other skilled workers — painter Mr Seefeld, locksmith and boilerman Mr Günther (when I arrived in 1920 they were the actual 'boiler house crew'; we were then joined by Dr Kostitscheff, the lady who sharpened the woodcarving tools, and for a short period Mr Gustl Hagmann, trained as a painter to assist me, and from about 1921 Mr Bollinger, electrician from Basel). People who had a special relationship with this 'boiler house crew' were tinsmith Mr Dollinger from Reinach, because of his trade, and bricklayer Mr Gienger who often came to ask for insulation tape for his hands burned by concrete mix and from whom we also needed concrete mix for our dowels. Mr Dollinger had his plumbing workshop in the north eastern part of the Goetheanum ground floor (below the scenery store); Mr Seefeld's paint store was next to this.

Mr von Heydebrandt who worked in arts and crafts was often working in the boiler house at the time. His original intention was to cut the number plates for the seats in the auditorium mechanically, but he later cut them by hand after all and made the raised figures on them. He would quite often make jewellery in the boiler house after work, and a pleasant friendship developed that continues to this day, when we meet. But he cannot really be said to have been one of the 'workers'. Mr Jan Stuten was someone else we, the 'boiler house crew', especially Mr Seefeld and Mr Günther, were friends with, for he wanted to have a brass band. In the evenings the boiler house would therefore often resound with the music Mr Günther played on his trombone and Mr Seefeld on one of his horns. My own efforts to produce a harmonious sequence of sounds on a bass tuba were in vain.

During the morning break and at lunch time a chessboard would usually be set up in Günther and Seefeld's small room so that they might give each other battle. But my ears would be more violently assailed by disputes over anthroposophical issues between the two, who were long-standing members. How often did I not feel: 'But surely they are both saying the same thing!' They would always make their peace again. Now these two are no longer on the physical plane.

The building work was directed by Mr Aisenpreis, the architect. In the architects' office, Mr Ranzenberger would be making his drawings. The wages office or financial department was run by Mr Binder. All of this was in the Glass House, as were the baths, looked after by Miss Stolle in addition to her other work. Before this, Miss Stolle (one of my mother's sisters) and others had been engraving the coloured glass windows in the Glass House. Later on nightwatchman Umber's watch dogs were also in the Glass House (he had been a confectioner before and at Christmas would bake *stollen* for us, a wonderful cake from Saxony, using his own special recipe—but only if Miss Stolle had collected orders for seven *stollen*; he would not bake less). Mrs Binder was running the canteen at the time; her son, Mr Ehrenfried Pfeiffer (who was studying chemistry in Basel) had taken responsibility for setting up the stage lighting and was my immediate superior.

So that was the human environment at the time, or at least my own subjective impression of it. In August and September 1920, before the course for university students was given, there was tremendous activity in the hut behind Friedwart House. Mr Willy Storrer had taken on the work of organizing the course, under the guidance of Dr Boos, and my mother, and after working hours also myself, were helping to run off copies of printed materials. Mr Storrer organized a shorthand course in the further education hut, with lessons given daily before work (I recall dear, big Miss Leetius saying: 'Well, I can write it all right, but not to read it.'). Paper was cut in strips on the Goetheanum stage to fill the 'straw palliasses' for the guests of the 'currency hospital' (students from countries with weak currencies).

The huge curtains were sewn on the stage, using an electrical sewing machine.

Yes, and after the course for university students the lectures Dr Boos was giving to the workers came to an end, and work just went on for a long time. We workers were a very different social stratum compared to the 'artists' who were busily carving wood or stone, and to the 'members' who would move around in floating purple garments, asking for the lights to be turned on in the dome (12,000 candlepower) so that they might 'meditate', and so on. We were supposed to take our number plaques from a board at the 'bosses' every morning, and put them back when we left. Some of the workers would look all around to see if 'it was OK' before they would take a breather, and if something went wrong the bosses would shout at them … Can you understand that things went against the grain among workers who were also members or younger workers or some who had caught the spirit of the time (various 'workers' councils', student councils, etc. had developed in 1918, 1919)?

I myself, and I think the rest of the 'boiler house crew', too, would keep my 'dog tag' in my pocket. I felt myself responsible for my own work, both in what I did and when I did it. If I was still lying in the sun under an apple tree after the mid-morning or midday break and a 'boss' came walking past, I'd stay where I was; I'd do my work, but in my own time … There was some tension. Did the social impulses of which one heard so much at that 'threefolding time' not apply at the Goetheanum of all places? What purpose was the 'temple' meant to serve? The unusual forms, the paintings of human history in the domes, the strange figures (stars, angels, demons) in the glass windows ... we were asked to help to build it all. Surely it was only right that we should also understand what those things represented?

Such questions were sometimes discussed in the boiler house. Gradually there were seven of us 'revolutionary-minded people' (Günther, Seefeld, Bollinger, myself, Dr Kostitscheff, Dollinger, Erbsmehl) who said to ourselves: 'Something must be done.' One day I went and asked the workers to come to a meeting in the Limbude; the 'bosses' were not invited. The meeting came to be more stormy than planned, but our wishes began to take form: to have lectures again on the meaning and significance of these new things, getting rid of the 'dog tags', no more shouting and hitting from the bosses (an apprentice had received a slap in the face).

The next morning there was a lot of fuss from the 'bosses'. As usual, rumour had blown things out of proportion; it was said we had demanded that the bosses be dismissed.

The matter was taken to Dr Steiner. He invited everybody to come to the Schreinerei hall, let people tell him, asking questions quietly, until gradually it all became clear and the rumours had been reduced down to our three requests again. He then said we could certainly have question and answer sessions, he himself would be prepared to do this, during working hours, of course; the money for the build-ing had come from donations but he felt this would be reasonable.

He also said the number plaques did not have to be hung on the board any more, and slaps should certainly not be given either. But as to the 'shouting', we should just hear how he, too, could sometimes shout like anything, for instance at the eurythmists, and we should not take it too seriously. (They had frequently gone in and out through the windows of their rehearsal room on the ground floor rather than come past Mr Kellermüller at the south entrance, and when Dr Steiner heard of this he had bars put on the windows, so that it would not happen again that a window was left open at night. Arson was nevertheless committed later on.)

He then discussed with us which part of the day would be best for our questions or for lectures—at 7 a.m., when work started, people were not yet sufficiently awake; at the end of the working day they would be too tired, before their midday meal too hungry, afterwards not so well able to take things in. The best time—for it would immediately follow a break from work—would be the hour after the mid-morning break.

And that is what happened. Every week that Rudolf Steiner was in Dornach we would have one or occasionally two 'workers' lectures', all based on questions asked by individuals among us. As a result the questions came from all kinds of areas (social issues, current topics such as the theory of relativity or rejuvenation treatments, art, religion, history, earth evolution, beekeeping, the guardian angel's warnings against dangers, alcoholism, nutrition, spiritualism, in any order, depending on when someone took heart and put his question). The way they were answered took us through all ages and places in this world. Things members would only discuss among themselves in an almost furtive manner, shrouding them in mystery, for instance the two Jesus children, would be considered freely and openly by Rudolf Steiner when he spoke to us, only few of whom were 'members' at that time (Günther, Seefeld, Erbsmehl, I think; I had become one since, and Bollinger and probably also Dollinger and others became members later), and it all made so much sense!

We were grateful to Dr Steiner for the love he showed us and for the wisdom he revealed, opening our eyes. He in turn was pleased to hear our questions and that he was able to speak to us. And I knew many occasions when he would take up a subject about which he had spoken to us in the morning in the members' lecture he gave in the evening, the subject being one of current concern. But he also spoke to us in a very special way—clearly, openly and simply, using examples that were striking, almost rough and ready, but always giving full value to the most profound things, not 'popularizing' them or being didactic. One cannot really describe his way, but readers of the printed lectures may perhaps get some idea of what I mean. He would be very straightforward, speaking as one of us—maybe one could put it like that. And yet we had an enormous respect for him, most of us would speak with trepidation, and discussions as to who should ask a question (speaking for the others) and which question often went on for days.

Perhaps you'd also like to know how it came about that these questions and answers later also came to be recorded in writing so that it was then possible to publish them. This was due to some ladies who were working behind the stage in the mornings, getting the eurythmy veils ready or the like, for instance Mrs Finkh, Miss Stolle, Mrs Mitscher. I do not know who asked Dr Steiner, but one day he told us that a request had been made by this group of people, asking if it might not be permitted to record these lectures as well (Dr Steiner's other lectures had been taken down in writing for years), because they offered so many aspects, often quite new ones.

And now something quite magnificent happened. Dr Steiner did not want to make the decision himself but asked us if we would agree! He felt that the questions we, the workers, brought, and the longing in our hearts, were so much our own affair, offering his answers wholly as a gift to us, that he did no longer feel they were his property and a matter for him to decide. And if just one of us had said he would find this embarrassing, Dr Steiner would certainly have refused permission. We did agree, and he then told the lady who wrote them down to sit behind the curtain so that we would not feel in any way inhibited.

Perhaps I may also add something that has been told to me by Mr Walther Cloos.

He said that Dr Steiner said about these workers' lectures that in them he was at last able to speak 'scientifically', something he found harder to do with the members. And it is in fact true that whilst it can be relatively difficult to relate the contents of the workers' lectures to the early books and lectures without finding contradictions, it is relatively easy to reconcile them with scientific facts. Scientific hypotheses may sound very different, but serious scientists are usually aware of the borderline between fact and hypothesis. We are thus able to find good material in the workers' lectures when considering borderline problems in the scientific world from the anthroposophical point of view, something which is extremely necessary in view of the rapid pace of change in the fields of physics and chemical technology. Physics and chemistry to be made wholly Christian—that was our teacher's heart's desire!

Finally an anecdote. If I remember rightly it was told to me by Dr Lehrs.

One day it was necessary to fit yet another meeting into Dr Steiner's full agenda. Someone is reported to have suggested a time when a workers' lecture was planned, using the words: '... after all, it's only a workers' lecture!' Dr Steiner is said to have replied, quite upset: 'Only? Only? ... the workers' lectures are most important!'

Notes

Text source. The lectures were taken down by Helene Finkh (1883–1960), a professional stenographer, and written out in cleartext by her. For the 3rd German edition (1981) on which this translation is based the original shorthand record has been completely reviewed and a new cleartext produced. Changes in the text compared to earlier German editions would be due to this.

GA = *Gesamtausgabe* (German edition of the collected works of Rudolf Steiner).

1 Incidents that had aroused ill feeling were discussed with the builders on 9 January, with further discussions following on 12 and 16 January.

2 Steiner, R., *Nine Lectures on Bees* (in GA 351), lecture of 12 December 1923. Tr. C.A. Meir, M. Pease. Spring Valley: St George 1975.

3 Steiner, R., *Nine Lectures on Bees* (see note 2), lecture of 15 December 1923.

4 Steiner, R., *The Human Being in Body, Soul and Spirit; Our Relationship to the Earth* (GA 347), lecture of 16 September 1922. Tr. J. Reuter and S. Seiler. New York: Anthroposophic Press & London: Rudolf Steiner Press 1989.

5 See notes 2 and 3.

6 For instance, Steiner, R., in *Cosmic Workings in Earth and Man* (in GA 350), lecture of 22 Sept 1923. Tr. V.E. Evans. London: Rudolf Steiner Publishing Co. 1952.

7 Steiner, R., *Health and Illness*, vol. 2 (in GA 348), lecture of 8 January 1923. Tr. M. St Goar. New York: Anthroposophic Press 1981 and 1983.

8 See note 6.

9 Marienbad, spa, in what was formerly Bohemia.

10 Marienquelle, Our Lady's Well.

11 Translator's note. Rudolf Steiner handled the gender of this person in an unusual way in the German. 'Albino' is a masculine noun in German. It is, however, normal usage to change to the feminine gender for any pronouns that follow if the individual is female. Rudolf Steiner did not do so. The text thus reads: 'was showing himself in all kinds of fair booths ... and he said ... he could not see well.' Rudolf Steiner was also using a term for an albino that was then colloquial in German: Kakerlak, meaning 'cockroach', which no doubt arose because cockroaches are also very sensitive to light.

12 Kolisko, L., *Milzfunktion und Plättchenfrage*. Dornach 1921.

13 Parathyroid glands (epithelial bodies). Mentioned in lecture given on 2 December 1922. GA 348.

14 Raphael Santi, 1483–1520.
    Leonardo da Vinci, 1452–1519.

15 See lecture of 23 January in this volume.

16 Reported in v. Schubert, GH., *Die Geschichte der Seele*, S. 539. 2. Aufl. Stuttgart 1833.

17 A weekly paper (in German) started by Rudolf Steiner that is still being published today. The essays have since been published in Steiner, R., *Rudolf Steiner, an Autobiography* (GA 28). Tr. R. Stebbing. New York: Rudolf Steiner Publications 1977.

18 Usteri, A., Der Mohn, *Das Goetheanum*, 2. Jahrg., Nr. 39 vom 6 Mai 1923.

19 Einstein, Albert (1879–1955).

20 Alfred Gysi (1864–1957), professor and lecturer at, and one of the founders of, Zurich University Institute of Dentistry. See also Steiner, R., *Der Wert des Denkens für eine den Menschen befriedigende Erkenntnis*, S. 48–49, Basel 1958 (The Value of Thinking for a Knowledge Satisfying to Man [in GA 164]). Tr. V.E. Watkin. Typescript, Rudolf Steiner House Library, London. Rudolf Steiner was thinking of writing a book on embryology in collaboration with Prof. Gysi.

21 Potatoes are only bad in the mouth. Those are the words recorded in German. Translator.

22 Copernicus, Nicolaus (1473–1543), Polish astronomer who established the view that the earth and the other planets orbit the sun.

23 See M. Wilhelm Meyer, *Die Gesetze der Bewegungen am Himmel und ihre Erforschung*, Berlin, n.d. On page 96 he says (in German): The only thing we know, incidentally, is that this total motive energy of the stars is currently taking our solar system through the universe and towards Hercules at a rate of some 30 kilometres a second, towards an unknown, dark destination that is infinitely far away for us.

24 Newton, Sir Isaac (1642–1727).

25 Reference to an experiment named after the Belgian physicist J.A.F. Plateau (1801–83).